# Praise for *The Decisive Element*

*The Decisive Element* celebrates the influence of leadership at every level in the school setting and highlights the importance of establishing and maintaining positive relationships with staff and students.

With its reflection on how inspirational leaders create the positive emotional climate that is so vital in promoting well-being, this book is a must-read for all those who want to 'bring out the sunshine' in their schools.

> Yvonne Cashmore, Senior Lecturer and PGCE Economics and Business Subject Lead, University of Worcester

*The Decisive Element* is not so much about sunny weather returning to our classrooms but more a convincing claim that it has never gone away.

Quite rightly too, as Gary, Mick and Chris demonstrate from their collective experience: they have taught so many lessons and led so many initiatives that every chapter, including those on motivation and leadership, echoes with authority and common sense. The authors also share and link back to classroom practice an impressive store of research and theory, but it's the warmth of the personal anecdotes that gives the book originality.

Teachers may well read *The Decisive Element* in one session, and will return to the classroom energised to spread more positive weather!

> Bob Cox, education consultant and author of the award winning Opening Doors to Quality Writing series

At a time when many in the media are declaring a mental health crisis in our schools, there has never been such a need for positivity among those of us who work in education. We need to change the narrative, and this very readable book provides an excellent starting point – sounding an essential call to action for all teachers to focus on the positive and to recognise the good that is happening around them.

Packed with sage advice, and written with the unique combination of wit and wisdom so typical of the authors, *The Decisive Element* offers a wealth of practical

tips to help you build better relationships, reap the rewards of positivity in your classroom and become the ultimate 'weather god' in your own school. There is great guidance here for new teachers on how to provide meaningful and impactful praise, and plenty of thought provoking exercises to challenge the practice of even the most experienced of practitioners. And all of this from accomplished school leaders who ooze credibility and authority having been there, done it all and worn the t-shirts.

There is not a teacher or educator in the land, whether experienced or newly qualified, who would not benefit from picking up *The Decisive Element*.

Andrea Taylor, Director, South Bromsgrove High Teaching School

As a school leader I try to never lose sight of the enormous impact that my demeanour can have on up to 750 people every single day, and smiling and treating people with dignity is so infectious. This brilliant book, backed up by theory and packed with practical tips that anybody can use, offers an entertaining reminder of why we do what we do, and challenges us to do it even better.

*The Decisive Element* should be essential reading for anybody who works in a school – highly recommended!

Jon Mellor, Head Teacher, Limehurst Academy

It's difficult to disagree with any of the sentiments and ideas in *The Decisive Element*. Filled with unique, real-life examples of how all those who work in schools contribute to make a difference to others and their learning, it highlights how every action we take with pupils over time has a profound impact on their overall development and well-being. And if we are to continue making 'that' difference in young people's lives, we need to put the philosophy the authors share in this book into action.

Essential reading – whether you are a classroom assistant, an experienced teacher, a school leader or simply considering going into teaching.

Tim J. Sutcliffe, Executive Head, Glen Hills Primary School

**Gary Toward**, **Mick Malton** and **Chris Henley**

I have come to a frightening conclusion that I am

The **DECISIVE**
**ELEMENT**

in the classroom

It is my personal approach that creates the climate

As a teacher I possess tremendous power to make a child's life miserable or joyous

I can be a tool of torture or an instrument of inspiration

I can humiliate or humor ... it is my response that

decides whether a child is humanized or de-humanized

It is my daily mood that

makes the weather

## Unleashing Praise and Positivity in Schools

Crown House Publishing Limited
www.crownhouse.co.uk

Published by
Crown House Publishing
Crown Buildings, Bancyfelin, Carmarthen, Wales, SA33 5ND, UK
www.crownhouse.co.uk
and
Crown House Publishing Company LLC
PO Box 2223, Williston, VT 05495, USA
www.crownhousepublishing.com

British Library of Cataloguing-in-Publication Data
A catalogue entry for this book is available from the British Library.

Print ISBN 978-178583312-0
Mobi ISBN 978-178583356-4
ePub ISBN 978-178383357-1
ePDF ISBN 978-178583358-8

LCCN 2018943080

Printed and bound in the UK by
TJ International, Padstow, Cornwall

# Contents

# Foreword

Five teachers changed my life.

Literally.

I was a child living in a home full of chaos, and their unconditional positive regard for me led to a gradual increase in self-belief that interrupted my trajectory towards a life on the streets.

Yes. That's the difference teachers make. What you do can't be measured in an observation lesson or served up as a neat little bundle of data for Ofsted – it's so much bigger than that.

It starts with a connection, which can be as simple as a smile but might not even be that.

Mrs Cook was permanently happy. Smiling, exuding love and positivity in that special way only those Everyday Heroes who spend their days surrounded by 5-year-olds can.

Mr Readman saw the funny side of everything. He was committed to fun and could flip any challenge into an opportunity for joy.

Mr Williams, Mr Simpson and Miss Archer were different. Not stern or cold but more partial to a firm handshake than a hug!

And yet each of them changed my mind about who I was by building a relationship that allowed a broken little girl to trust.

See, it's not what you say and do but what you think and feel that comes through. Especially for children like me growing up in an abusive home. I can read authenticity a mile off and that's great news! If you're not a Tigger type, it's not about faking joy but about feeling joy – in whatever form that takes. When you are authentic it shows, and it speaks volumes and makes deposits in our emotional bank accounts.

The authors of this book are gloriously weird (compared to how completely normal I am), and yet from the moment I heard them speak, I knew we shared a sense of the transformative power of who teachers are in the classroom.

It might feel like the government, Ofsted or the sword of Damocles is hanging over your capacity to impact the lives of the mini humans in front of you, but the truth is that you have more agency than you know.

And it starts with remembering that the best thing about you is that you are a human who cares.

For a roadmap to the rest, read on.

Jaz Ampaw-Farr

# Introduction

What makes a great school? There has long been a national conversation about our education system, and of course everyone is an expert, because they all went to school! Conversations abound about types of school, school buildings, settings, uniforms, exams, league tables … the list is endless. Usually, suggested changes are costly and schools are always limited by money. What lies behind this book is the belief that it is people who make the difference. Teachers and school leaders make the weather in every classroom and in every school, and it is their mindset which transforms lives, for ever, helped and assisted by each and every adult who works in a school. They are all educators.

All three of us have made speeches on the day of a colleague's leaving or retirement, and we have always ensured that such events were happy, positive, upbeat and fun. Equally, we have all had the honour of speaking at funerals, sharing life-affirming stories about the departed person and praising their legacy. On these occasions, it's easy to find things to be positive about, even though everyone we have eulogised will have messed up at some point. However, it seems that, increasingly, many folks are quick to pick up on negative things and resort to moaning, complaining or saying unpleasant things about others.

It's so effortless in our modern, speedy, Internet driven society to add off-the-cuff complaints and moans to social media posts – an article by Leo Kelion reveals the ' "worrying" amount of hate speech' that children are exposed to online.[1] Our mate Andy Cope reckons that 'Most people nestle comfortably in the bottom third' of a positivity graph, while around 2%

---

1    Leo Kelion, 'Children see "worrying" amount of hate speech online', *BBC News* (16 November 2016). Available at: http://www.bbc.co.uk/news/technology-37989475.

spend most of their time in the top third.[2] Andy calls these folk 2%ers, and it is our view that it is these people who make the difference in any organisation because they are habitually positive and have a huge impact on everyone else.

While we understand that the world can be a challenging place and that life is full of trials and tribulations, we'd like to think there's a way that we can all get the best out of each other and actually feel happier and more successful – to help each other be the best versions of ourselves. The 2%ers see problems just like everyone else, but instead of jumping into doom and gloom mode, they look for a positive way forward and search for solutions. This is not to say that they never have a down time; of course they do. But positive people bounce back because of the way they choose to be, and it is this way of thinking that we want to tap into.

The awesome poet and civil rights activist Maya Angelou is reputed to have seen it this way: 'I've learned that people will forget what you said, people will forget what you did, but people will never forget how you made them feel.'

This book is aimed at teachers and school staff of all kinds; from reception class to sixth form, state and fee paying, to university and further education. Whatever your context – inner city, leafy suburb or rural – we don't claim, or aim, to have the magic elixir to help you get everyone you teach into the top third of the positivity stakes. But we do have more than a few things to say about what we could all do to help the young people we lead to get the most out of life.

We refer to teachers, we refer to support staff and we refer to school leaders. However, let's clear this up now: everyone working in a school is a leader of some sort. Teachers and classroom assistants lead the learning; office staff lead in the engine room of the school and in their relationships

---

2   Andy Cope and Andy Whittaker, *The Art of Being Brilliant: Transform Your Life by Doing What Works for You* (Chichester: Capstone, 2012), p. 26.

with the pupils, staff and parents; middle leaders, coordinators and senior leaders drive the direction and dynamics of the school curriculum. In the staffroom, whoever is talking is leading while others listen. How this all happens matters hugely because everything that takes place in schools boils down to outcomes for pupils.

Some folk are a real pleasure to be with most of the time. Some bosses you'd follow anywhere. Some you might wish would read this book and apply it to their world. Some teachers have the most challenging kids[3] eating out of the palm of their hand and others struggle with fairly compliant classes. So, why is it that one teacher can inspire and at the same time challenge a class of teenagers or 7-year-olds, while another teacher might struggle with the same group? We will explore these strange happenings and ask why certain teachers inspire kids, help them to make leaps in learning, engage them and pull off the Maya Angelou trick – make them feel good.

Maya Angelou's maxim is a great starting point. In the course of any one day you could easily have hundreds of different interactions with other human beings. If you add in the social media mix you could be talking thousands, even millions. Cast your mind back over yesterday. How many people do you think you communicated with in one way or another? What did you say? What did you do? How much of this was with the youngsters you teach? The exact detail may well be irrelevant, but the effect of your saying and doing is anything but. So, in saying and doing what you said and did yesterday, how many of the hundreds or thousands do you think felt good because of it?

Words and actions can be hastily assembled and subtle differences in tone, phrasing or body language can easily give the recipient the wrong

---

3   We will use a variety of names for the young folk we teach. 'Kids' is commonly used in schools so we'll also use it here. But whatever your common terms are, our youngsters are the most important folk in this story, so please feel free to think of them in your own terms.

message, leaving them feeling very different to how we actually want them to feel. If you live in that bottom third of positivity for most of your life, then the chances are that your communication will often have a negative effect on others. Being negative requires little effort, whereas investing in a positive way to influence the lives of others requires much more commitment and thought. As we observed earlier, everyone sees problems, but the big difference here is that it is easy to simply moan, groan, carp and whinge about whatever the issue happens to be. However, to switch from a negative to positive attitude, takes time, effort and thought. When we do, though, we can transform the situation from a problem to an opportunity. These are the folk who become weather gods.

Let's pause at this point as we don't want to offend anyone. We are going to refer to 'weather gods' repeatedly, and when we do so we are talking about non-gender-specific, all-powerful deities in schools. We are alluding to the following quote by Haim Ginott:

> I have come to a frightening conclusion. I am the decisive element in the classroom. It is my personal approach that creates the climate. It is my daily mood that makes the weather. As a teacher I possess tremendous power to make a child's life miserable or joyous. I can be a tool of torture or an instrument of inspiration. I can humiliate or humor, hurt or heal. In all situations it is my response that decides whether a crisis will be escalated or de-escalated, and a child humanized or de-humanized.[4]

Teachers, then, are the weather gods of the classroom. Brilliant teachers bring the sun in with them as they arrive, they fill their classrooms with joy and laughter and, for most of the time (notice we are not saying all of the time), their pupils want to do what they want them to do. Such teachers are boomerang teachers – the ones the kids want to come back to for more. The ones pupils ask when they see them at breaktime in the yard, 'Have

---

4   Haim G. Ginott, *Teacher and Child: A Book for Parents and Teachers* (New York: Macmillan, 1972), pp. 15–16.

*I have come to a frightening conclusion. I am the decisive element in the classroom. It is my personal approach that creates the climate. It is my daily mood that makes the weather. As a teacher I possess tremendous power to make a child's life miserable or joyous. I can be a tool of torture or an instrument of inspiration. I can humiliate or humor, hurt or heal. In all situations it is my response that decides whether a crisis will be escalated or de-escalated, and a child humanized or de-humanized.*

we got you next, Miss?' or 'Are we making our volcanoes this afternoon, Sir?' These are the teachers who in thirty years' time will be shopping in Sainsbury's (other supermarkets are available) when, while perusing the incredibly wide selection of tomatoes, a voice will grab their attention: 'Hello, Miss.' They will be greeted like a long lost friend and told how much they made a difference to that person when they were young. They might even mention how much they helped them in a particular way – something the teacher didn't even know about at the time.

This is one of the great things about being a teacher. Forget data, forget Ofsted ('Oh we wish we could!' we hear you cry), forget league tables. What really matters are the little human beings who teachers help to become adults and, for most of the time, the help goes unnoticed by everyone but the child. Unless you happen to have a chance meeting next to the tomatoes, you may never know, but trust us: when you make a difference to a child, you never un-make that difference and sometimes it can be life changing. These teachers are MAD! Yes, MAD – they Make A Difference.

This is why being a weather god is so important because every difference needs to be a good one. If we could create a generation of kids who all had positive memories of every teacher they encountered, then we really would unleash the power of the weather gods.

We're guessing – no, hoping – that because you've picked up this book, and you're reading it, you don't actively spend your days thinking up ways of making others feel unhappy. We hope that you have the ambition to make young people feel great about themselves and to help them become the best they can be. We guess that you are either an aspirational weather god or already well on your way to being one. If that's the case, this book's for you.

We hope you enjoy it.

Chapter 1

# The Big R: Creating the Climate in School

It is our huge privilege now to visit a wide selection of schools across the UK. One thing we have learned is that postcode is absolutely no indicator of what we will find when we arrive. We have turned up to schools in what look like salubrious and favourable surroundings, only to find ourselves feeling uncomfortable; equally, we have been to schools in altogether more challenging contexts where we have been bowled over by the warmth of our reception and the buzz of the institution.

We ask ourselves time and time again, what is the difference? What is the indefinable quality which makes one school distinct from another? If you ask a lay person the same question, they will often cite the head as the determining factor. A school can surge up and down the fickle barometer of local opinion and reputation according to the perceived effectiveness of the head teacher. We think this is a bit restrictive because our experience tells us that being part of a successful school is a huge team effort; there is never just one superhero but a phalanx of dedicated and skilled professionals. But whether we ascribe the perceived success to one person or to a wider team, what is for sure is that great schools have great leaders who make the weather on a daily basis. It is all about that big R: *Relationships*. Of necessity this will start at the top: in creating the weather, great leaders will be the source of the feel-good waterfall which cascades positivity, inspiration and self-belief to every stakeholder. In great schools this is true of every single member of staff because, as we shall see, we are all leaders.

School improvement is constantly on the agenda in schools, and the government of the day will make it its business to oversee this process. In a democracy where the taxpayer foots the bill this is a fact of life, but we reckon that it is in the DNA of everyone who works with kids to want to improve all the time. None of us reaches the pot of gold at the end of the rainbow where everything is sorted. Policies, procedures and protocols – many of which will be massively draining on time, money and energy – will abound to make the system ever more rigorous, robust and transparent. We contend that one of the most effective ways of transforming a school is to change the mindset of every person in the establishment. And it starts at the top with a single-minded drive to inspire everyone, employee and young person, to aspire to be the best possible at all times. Inspiration, aspiration and no small amount of perspiration will open up new frontiers of achievement across the board, and it costs nothing – a zero-cost route to school improvement. It is all down to leadership – great leaders who create the weather for everyone by building quality relationships and enabling fantastic teamwork. Put simply, leaders who are weather gods.

Chris attended the funeral of an elderly relative recently, and during the eulogy the son of the deceased described his mother's role in developing healthcare in the town in which she had lived in the mid-1960s. He told the congregation that his mother's theme tune could have been the Frank Sinatra classic, 'My Way', to which he added that she had made a passable attempt at ensuring that everyone else did it her way as well. She was a formidable contributor to making this world a better place. She was not a domineering person; indeed, she had a kindly and gracious manner. But she also had a steely determination to get done what she set out to get done and an inimitable ability to persuade people that it was in their interest, and also within their capacity, to do what she wanted. Put simply, she made people believe they could do it.

So, how? On her journey through life, what sort of qualities did she and others like her have? How can we learn from them to get the best out of people? How do we get other people to do what we want them to do, or even better, how do we get them to *want* to do what we want them to do (because once they want to do it the battle is at least half won)? How do we get teenage children to tidy their rooms? How do we encourage members of a club or group to play a fuller part? How do we get work colleagues for whom we bear a leadership responsibility to go the extra mile? How do we persuade those who are inclined to be cussed and resistant to conform and buy in?

Great leadership has fascinated and intrigued all three of us. We have worked for leaders who were an absolute pleasure. They were supportive and understanding but at the same time they had that knack of taking us outside our comfort zone and inspiring us to take the risks which enhanced and enriched our development as people and as colleagues. They helped us to become better teachers too, so the kids benefitted as well. Equally, we have all encountered those who were shrill and critical. Woe betide you if you slipped up or fell short. They ruled with a rod of iron and had an eagle eye for any shortcomings. They seemed to be constantly looking for failure and errors, no matter how small. If you work or live with anyone like this, you'll know that you spend a lot of time looking over your shoulder.

When Gary began his teaching career, the leader of the faculty where he worked was made in this mould, and on his first day in the job he witnessed his new boss wielding his power. At the beginning of the year he would gather together all the new pupils attending lessons in his faculty to establish the ground rules. They all trotted in bright eyed and bushy tailed, fresh in their new uniform, clutching new bags and new pencil cases containing new pens and pencils. They came in and sat down while the teachers, including Gary, stood around the edge of the room.

The king of this castle then began his address to the pupils by asking them what they thought they should bring to the lessons in *his* area. Hands popped up and there were plenty of willing participants eager to share in this new and exciting secondary school world. What a mistake! Typically, the exchange went like this:

> *Leader: So, everyone, what should you bring to these lessons?*
>    (points at enthusiastic child with hand up)

*Child* (smiling)*: Pen and pencil.*

*Leader* (with a glare)*: Pardon?*

*Child* (with an uncertain smile)*: Pen and pencil.*

*Leader* (still glaring)*: Pardon?*

*Child* (looking uncomfortable and face reddening)*: Pen and pencil.*

*Leader* (even sterner and frowning)*: Pardon?*

(Child begins to cry, not knowing what to say.)

This went on until either the child twigged or someone whispered to them that they needed to use the word 'Sir'. However, it would continue as the next question was asked: 'What else should you bring to these lessons?' It may have been the pressure of the situation but not all of the kids worked out what was happening, and typically this scenario played out repeatedly until several bewildered children had been reduced to tears and the lucky others looked on aghast, probably feeling anything but excited about this new school. This colleague was certainly a weather god, but a herald of storm and hurricane rather than sunshine and light. A leader who ruled by fear.

Gary remembers cringing inwardly as he watched this spiteful scene unfold. What did those kids feel like now? Would they look forward to coming to school tomorrow? It was then that he began to think that the type of education he'd been through himself (with caning, slippering and rulers across the knuckles) and the version of 'discipline' he'd just witnessed was not the approach he wanted to dish out himself.

In this case, Gary was witnessing a teacher as the leader of a group of kids, but we have seen school leaders treat their team members in a similar way. Chris had a conversation at the end of a training course recently with a lunchtime supervisor who said that she had felt ritually belittled by the senior leadership in a school where she had given eighteen years of service, constantly being made to feel like a second-class citizen. There has to be a better way.

We would like to put it to you that no matter how much you shout at someone or punish them – whether it be at home or in school – you will never instil in them a passion to wholeheartedly engage in what you want them to do. We'd bet our last £22.56 that you'll not find a pupil saying, 'That detention last night has really given me a passion for reading more Shakespeare!' We think quite the opposite. (That'll be £22.56 you owe us, by the way!)

Mick recalls how, in his early thirties, he played for a football team with a teammate who constantly shouted at him and the other players if they made an error. Now, you may not have met Mick but let's just say he isn't shy of telling folk if they are out of order. So, Mick did something the little schoolboy Mick might not have done. At the end of a game he took the player to one side and asked him if he really thought that shouting at him would make him want to play better or put in more effort for the team. He explained that shouting demotivated him and made him less likely to do well, and that a little positive encouragement might go a long way. Now, you'll be hoping at this point that the shouty player came to the next match having changed his ways, full of super encouragement and positivity. Nope, sadly that wasn't the outcome, but what did happen was that the chap didn't shout at Mick any more and Mick was able to get on with his game without the burden of being 'told off' repeatedly.

There are those who take delight in this ruthless, authoritarian style of leadership, and a few – but only a few – for whom it achieves results. Leadership does, of course, require courage, resolve and the commitment to challenge underperformance. However, it is our experience, and that of others across the world, that the leaders who really get the best out of people are not those who rule by fear and by cracking the whip; it is those who understand every tiny detail of what makes each team member tick and how to get the best out of them. This is a key focus of the book, so let's take a look at leadership, drawing on some super research to help us find our way.

## Clever stuff

A great deal of research and theorising has been carried out into leadership. This is as true in the field of education as it is in business. It is helpful for all leaders, be they of the experienced, developing or aspirational variety, to remind themselves of the theory behind leadership styles. A brief look into the development of leadership style theory can help to stimulate reflection and enable leaders to keep on developing as they learn how to lead. This is just as important for school leaders in the business of education as it is for business leaders in the world of commerce.

One of the very early pioneers in the research and development of leadership styles was American psychologist Kurt Lewin. He led a team of researchers in the 1930s who undertook experiments into leadership styles in the field of decision making. The experiments were carried out with groups of schoolchildren who were observed being led in different ways for an arts and crafts project. Their findings have helped to form the basis for much of the subsequent development of leadership style theory.[1]

From this early work, Lewin identified three leadership styles:

+   **Autocratic** – tight control over the group and its activities, where the leader typically takes decisions without consulting others in the team, even if their input might be useful. In the experiment, the researchers found that this style of leadership caused the greatest level of discontent and decision making was less creative.

---

1   Kurt Lewin, Ronald Lippit and Ralph K. White, 'Patterns of aggressive behaviour in experimentally created social climates', *Journal of Social Psychology* 10(2) (1939): 271–301.

+ **Democratic** – where the leader involves other team members in the decision making process, although the way the decision is finally made may vary from a process of consensus to the leader listening to views and then having the final say. In Lewin's experiments this was found to be the most successful style.

+ **Laissez-faire** – low levels of control by the leader, whose role in the decision making is kept to a minimum, thereby allowing group members to make their own decisions. In the experiments, the researchers found this group to be the least effective because they lost direction.

Since Lewin's early studies there has been plenty of subsequent research and theory which has resulted in some sophisticated thinking and writing on leadership styles. However, those early pioneering studies by Lewin and his colleagues have been very influential and helped to establish the three major leadership styles which we still recognise today:

+ **Authoritarian (autocratic)** – where leaders provide clear parameters for what they want, how they want it, when and by whom. This is based heavily on a command and control style. Authoritarian leadership can be best utilised in situations where there is little time for group decision making or when the situation calls for strong, swift and decisive action.

+ **Democratic** – which actively seeks to encourage contributions from the group. Done well, this kind of leadership can encourage participation, engagement, creativity and motivation.

+ **Delegative (laissez-faire)** – where leaders offer little guidance to the group, leaving it up to them to decide on the best actions. This can work well when there is no need to have a centrally coordinated action and when group members are capable of making their own decisions, perhaps within an agreed framework put forward by senior leadership. However, it can lead to drift and poorly defined roles, leading to inefficiency.

We believe it is essential for leaders at every level in schools to be excellent at leading; only then will they be able to establish the necessary positive and empathetic culture in their teams.

This piece of clever stuff is simply a brief introductory taster to whet the appetite for further investigation. We feel sure that investing time in understanding the theory and research behind the practice of leadership further will be time well spent.

In the world of sport, there are legendary figures who have taken over a position of leadership in a team and, without radically changing the nature or make-up of the team, have achieved dramatically improved results. During the 1981 Ashes series between England and Australia, Mike Brearley took over the captaincy from a faltering Ian Botham and the England team was transformed. Whereas previously Botham and Bob Willis were performing like run of the mill journeymen and England were being outplayed, almost overnight the team started to play out of their skins and the Ashes were won in a memorable summer of cricket. As we mention later, Eddie Jones enabled the recent England rugby team to perform a similar U-turn following their early World Cup exit in 2015. Boris Becker was instrumental in helping Novak Djokovic to rule the tennis world. Most recently, Tracey Neville has transformed the English netball team from perpetual also-rans to gold medal winners at the 2018 Commonwealth Games. None of these people suddenly unearthed geniuses; they worked with who they had but they got the best out of them by building strong and positive relationships. They changed the climate.

What did all these inspirational leaders have in common? They knew their players inside out, they understood what made them tick and they knew when to administer stern words – after all, the world of top flight professional sport is not for the faint-hearted. They also knew when to encourage, when to inspire and when to put the metaphorical hand on the shoulder and say, 'You can do it!'

# Positive Relationships

Schools are complex organisations with leaders scattered everywhere. Let's consider again the notion of everyone in a school being a leader. Gary often tells newly qualified and trainee teachers that they are leaders, and they often look slightly bemused. However, they lead in the classroom and every time they say or do something in school; a comment in the staffroom, their body language in the playground, how they greet parents in meetings. Every single member of staff creates the emotional climate in some way, and in the grand scheme everything distils down to the impact on children and how they feel.

How school staff feel has a natural impact on what happens in the class-room and in interactions with children. If a teacher can create fine weather in the classroom, then the head can blow warming winds across the whole school. The head of department, estate manager, special educational needs coordinator, head of year, form tutor and teaching assistant can all conjure up wonderful climates. We argue that every member of staff is a leader in some way as what they say and what they do will have an impact on how the people they work with feel. This also happens from the front of the school with the staff who meet and greet in reception. We like to call these folk 'directors of first impressions' because it is so important that they build positive relationships with everyone who enters the school. A cheery smile and some positive, warm words of welcome will create the weather and make an instant initial relationship with any visitor. The neg-ative person who holds court in the staffroom can be the opposite – a 'mood hoover' who sucks the positivity out of all in their path.[2] The posi-tive, cheery colleague who passes on their positivity is the antidote to such doom and gloom merchants.

Weather gods in schools take sunshine everywhere and build positive rela-tionships. They learn names and build knowledge about those they teach and the colleagues they work alongside. They create a feeling of warmth where both kids and colleagues benefit from feeling cared for and valued. They are the 2%ers who solve problems, create opportunities and see the positive in everyone.

They understand what it means to 'stroke the cat'. Let us pause for a min-ute and contemplate what happens as you start to stroke a cat's back: there is an instant reaction, a feel-good reflex, and you can almost sense the cat purring, 'Oooh, that's nice, give me some more of that!' The pampered puss will arch its back and ping its tail into an upright position in its appre-ciation of your ministrations. To pursue the analogy a little further for a moment, just consider what a cat's reaction is to being told off. Mick's next

---

2   See Gary Toward, Chris Henley and Andy Cope, *The Art of Being a Brilliant Teacher* (Carmarthen: Crown House Publishing, 2015).

door neighbours had a delightful black cat who committed murder most foul at the expense of a local sparrow and the poor moggy was confined to barracks for three days as punishment. Next time she was out and about yet another member of the local flock bit the dust. It's what cats do. They greet discipline and criticism with a nonchalant flick of the tail and an insouciant determination to ignore you. But stroking their backs? Now, that's a different thing altogether.

How does this translate into schools? To pretend that you are never going to be critical is the stuff of fantasy, but if the emphasis is tilted heavily in favour of seeing the good in people (or, indeed, in the potential for how they could be even better), then the results will be transformational for the individuals concerned, for the class and, ultimately, for the school. You need to make people believe that they can do it, that it is in their interests to do it and that they actually want to do it. Make them dare to dream and dreams can begin to become reality.

By contrast, approach the situation in an authoritative fashion and you are likely to achieve, at best, a sour atmosphere, a spirit of resentful compliance or an inclination to do just enough to keep out of further trouble. It doesn't take too much of a trip down memory lane to remember how we felt as children when we were told off. Our guess is that you dreaded it and that even now the idea of being berated by someone makes you recoil. In such a culture, team members jump high enough to reach the bar of expectation and avoid having to suffer a scolding, but they will rarely, if ever, jump high enough to raise the bar. No sporting team ever gained pre-eminence from simply reaching the bar of limited expectation. No school ever thrived and excelled under such duress. No family ever enjoyed the harmony of a happy home because of the fear instilled by an authoritative parent.

Thinking back to Lewin's study and the framework of what he identifies as authoritarian leadership, we suggest there is a distinction to be made between being authoritarian and being assertive. Being *assertive* certainly implies being determined about securing the outcome you have identified, relentless in its pursuit and clear about the stages needed to get there. Also implicit is an emotional intelligence which means that you understand the other person, acknowledge their strengths and make them feel good about themselves, but you are equally aware of where they may find the going tough and how you are going to help them. You make them dare to dream that they can succeed and inspire them to believe that this is for them. You have a vision of their potential, possibly seeing in them virtues and strengths which they may not see in themselves. You look at the rainbow and not the thunder cloud.

Members of your team will be worried about failure, not because they fear recrimination and punishment but because they fear they will let you down. Assertive leaders lead by example, setting their sights high, both for themselves and for the team. They have strategies in place to ensure success even when challenges are encountered, but above all they feed on a diet of constant and infinite positivity. They have a vision which they communicate to those they lead – like Daniel Barenboim, whose mission it is to find ways of enabling understanding between Arabs and Israelis to grow through the music of his West-Eastern Divan Orchestra.[3] He is driven by his passion for the cause of improving understanding between nations, and members of the orchestra join him on the journey, each with his or her individual part to play. It goes without saying that these are musicians of the highest quality, but it is more than musical expertise that binds them together. They play to audiences who are steeped in the clash of two cultures which dates back for centuries. Barenboim sees music as a way of bridging this tragic divide, of healing age old tensions and finding ways of uniting people where historically only confrontation and conflict have existed.

Mick remembers having two employees who were causing him some concerns. One had recently returned from maternity leave and was not really pulling her weight. At her best she was hardworking and reliable, one of the dependable folk in an organisation who help the wheels to turn on a

---

3   See Charles Phillips, *50 Leaders who Changed History* (New York: Quantum Books, 2015), pp. 212–214.

daily basis without ever being likely to take the world by storm, but her line manager had now raised some reservations about her commitment. A one-to-one was set up, and Mick started by asking her how she was finding it, juggling being a mum, childcare and her return to work. He went on to say how much he marvelled at how people managed these conflicting roles, recalling a couple of touching stories from when he was bringing up his own family. He then went on to express his admiration and praise for her personally, to offer any support he could as she settled back in, to thank her because he knew that he could count on her as a valued member of the team and to suggest a possible future development for her to undertake in due course. What he was doing was praising her for what he wanted her to do, to re-energise her self-belief in her contribution at work and to make her want to up her effort to justify his faith in her. The result: her commitment noticeably increased and she took on the new idea he had put to her within a matter of months. Bingo!

The other was a very talented guy whose body language always betrayed him. He had a perpetual air of being put upon, of everything being too much trouble, of wanting to be somewhere else, and yet when he propelled himself into action in his curriculum area, he was one of the most effective members of the team. Apparently even his mother used to say to him, 'Paul, you look like a miserable so-and-so!' Mick took him to one side and had a pretty frank exchange along the following lines: 'Paul, I hope you won't mind my saying so but you do come across as being negative, and there are those who fall for that image of you. I'm not one of them. As far as I'm concerned you are potentially the powerhouse of your area. You are the one who can make the others tick and you can raise the outcomes for the whole team. I rate you and I'm going to dig you out from behind that facade to become a leader of the pack.' He praised him for his potential and for what he wanted him to be and, guess what, Paul massively raised his game thereafter. What was critical was that the praise was genuine. False praise fools no one. Paul's faults were alluded to, so he could not dismiss this approach as soft soap, but he responded to Mick spotting his value and his talents. The outcome was good for him, good for the school and good for the people who really matter – the kids.

*Authoritarian* leaders are cast in a different mould. They are confrontational by instinct, using the power of their position to enforce conformity to their own standards and expectations. They can have an inflated sense of their own importance and resort to bullying tactics to ensure that their team follows them. Fear about the consequences of failure plays a major part in raising the work rate and contribution of each person. It was said of Frederick the Great that he wanted his soldiers to be more afraid of their commanding officers than of the enemy.[4] In every walk of life we know that there are leaders who rule by *force majeure*, and those they lead exist in a culture in which they expect to be criticised and to have fault found in them. They live in fear of that happening, so in order to avoid the worst penalties they work as hard and as well as they feel they can.

Chris recalls a conversation with a woman who had been a secretary in one of those big typing pools which were commonplace in many organisations in the 1970s. She remembered well her supervisor, Miss Richmond. Even in her sixties you could still discern the fear in her eyes at the mention of this harridan. All the typists would sit up that little bit straighter when she came into the room. They dreaded her peering over their shoulders and looking to pick up any inaccuracy or lapse in spelling or grammar. They were all terrified of getting something wrong. Does living and working in such a stressful and negative environment enable people to thrive, or merely to exist just above the threshold where chastisement and penalties are applied?

In the next chapter we will tell you about some research carried out by Gallup which links to our contention that if people are browbeaten into the best level of performance they think they can achieve, then they will never release the creative yeast to make the dough rise, whereby individuals

---

4    See Phillips, *50 Leaders who Changed History*, pp. 82–85.

discover strengths they did not know they had, with the result that the whole school achieves goals that are beyond its wildest dreams. It becomes a thriving, vibrant place, where pupils and staff alike love being. The key that unlocks this school's door is creating a culture and climate of positivity in which every person feels valued and recognised for the part they play. And it all begins with building positive relationships. While you might think that this is the responsibility of the head teacher, it's not. In a school, it's everyone's responsibility to build those relationships and create a positive focus because this changes kids' lives for the better.

## More clever stuff

There are probably as many different leadership styles as there are leaders, but fortunately research in this area has been able to offer us some key models. In particular, finding out how resonant and dissonant leadership operate is well worth the time spent for leaders at any level who want to develop their practice in the direction set out in this book. We offer just a very brief introduction here.

Any exploration of resonant leadership involves a keen reflection on the development of emotional intelligence – they are intrinsically linked. The main research on resonant and dissonant leadership has been carried out by Daniel Goleman, Richard Boyatzis and Annie McKee in the United States. Their findings appear in the influential book *Primal Leadership: Realizing the Power of Emotional Intelligence*, which they updated in 2013.[5]

---

5   Daniel Goleman, Richard Boyatzis and Annie McKee, *Primal Leadership: Realizing the Power of Emotional Intelligence* (Boston, MA: Harvard Business School Press, 2013). These ideas are explored more fully in Richard Boyatzis and Annie McKee, *Resonant Leadership* (Boston, MA: Harvard Business School Press, 2005) and Richard Boyatzis, Annie McKee and Frances Johnston, *Becoming a Resonant Leader: Develop Your Emotional Intelligence, Renew Your Relationships, Sustain Your Effectiveness* (Boston, MA: Harvard Business School Press, 2008).

A very useful summary of their ideas can be found in an online article by Daniel Goleman in which he describes resonant leadership beautifully:

> *Resonance means reinforcing sound by moving on the same wavelength. Leaders have the power to impact the emotional states of people around them. They can have a positive effect, pulling everyone onto the same upbeat wavelength. Or, they can create a dissonance, where their negativity bumps up against the emotions of others. Resonant leaders use their emotional intelligence to direct the feelings to help a group meet its goals.[6]*

In *Primal Leadership*, Goleman and his co-authors describe four styles of leadership that can help to create and build resonance in a group. These are visionary, coaching, affiliative and democratic, which he describes as follows in the same online article:

> *Visionary leaders see the big picture of where they're headed, share that perspective with the group, and inspire them to work together to reach their goals. …*
>
> *The coaching style of leadership happens most often in one-on-one interactions. This style focuses on the personal development of staff members. By showing genuine interest in individuals, this style helps leaders build trust and rapport. …*
>
> *The affiliative style of leadership is all about building relationships and collaboration. Using empathy, a core skill of emotional intelligence, affiliative leaders boost morale by valuing people and their feelings. …*

6   Daniel Goleman, 'Master the four styles of resonant leadership', *LinkedIn* (26 March 2016). Available at: https://www.linkedin.com/pulse/master-four-styles-resonant-leadership-daniel-goleman.

> *The democratic style of leadership draws on the knowledge of the group either to give input or to actually collaborate in making decisions.*

Moving forward, it might be helpful to reflect on your own practice and ask yourself if you think you have the empathy, self-awareness and emotional intelligence to master the four styles needed to be a resonant leader.

And what of dissonant leadership leading to a dissonant work environment? Such places are likely to be out of harmony, tense and even toxic to work in, which can lead to stress, frustration and disillusionment. Leaders in these environments might be viewed as cold and distant. It does not automatically follow that dissonant leaders have necessarily chosen to be that way. It may be that they lack the emotional intelligence and self-awareness needed to be successful resonant leaders. Dissonant leaders tend to be more authoritarian and operate by command and control structures. It should be added that this may well be exactly what is required in some scenarios when action needs to be taken urgently, perhaps in a crisis situation. However, it is our view in this book that a resonant work environment in schools will be more effective for the colleagues who work there and the pupils who go there to learn and grow.

## Top tips

- The big R – weather god leaders create positive relationships that underpin a thriving school community.

- Every person in a school creates the weather.

- Positivity is most likely to get people to want to do what you want them to do.

- Positive people can infect others with their positivity which also has an impact on the kids.

- Punishment, nagging and criticism is not likely to inspire.

- Focus on people's strengths and admirable qualities.

Chapter 2

# Making the Weather
# in the Classroom

In Chapter 1 we looked at leadership, but bear with us as we explore the topic a little more as you will soon see how it links directly to the classroom. We are also going to challenge you to try a few things you might not have thought of.

It may seem a bit of a conundrum that so many organisations appear to be led by people whose style is autocratic and lacking in empathy for those they lead. It seems like common sense that an approach which makes people feel valued and supported is more likely to be beneficial to the company. Gregory P. Smith identifies ten reasons why people leave their jobs and, astonishingly, each one begins with the word 'management'. Most of the reasons given would be avoidable with a different approach.[1] The *Harvard Business Review* is even more blunt, stating that 'In general, people leave their jobs because they don't like their boss …'[2]

This is not to say that an autocratic style of leadership is without its merits or that it can never succeed. Sometimes we have seen an autocratic leader, focused on bureaucracy and output, become successful very quickly. However, in our experience that success doesn't last because the people who 'do the doing' either become disenchanted by the lack of recognition or they simply leave as they feel undervalued. In fact, Gary found himself in exactly that position when his leader was so underwhelming that he decided to leave, but not before he was able to use the negative nature of

---

1    Gregory P. Smith, 'Why people quit their jobs', *Business Know-How* (20 May 2013). Available at: http://www.businessknowhow.com/manage/whyquit.htm.
2    *Harvard Business Review*, 'Why people quit their jobs' (20 September 2016). Available at: https://hbr.org/2016/09/why-people-quit-their-jobs.

the regime he was working in to help him form his own diametrically oppo-site approach. If it's difficult for an adult to work with, can you imagine how hard it is for a child who has a negative teacher?

## Clever stuff

The Gallup organisation has surveyed over four million employees on this very topic and what seems critical for anyone in leadership is that they don't forget to praise and the recognise the contributions people make to the organisation or team. In 2004, their research found that people who worked for positive and empathic leaders:

+ *increase their individual productivity*

+ *increase engagement among their colleagues*

+ *are more likely to stay with their organization*

+ *receive higher loyalty and satisfaction scores from customers*

+ *have better safety records and fewer accidents on the job*[3]

What stumps us is why this is not clear to those who appoint leaders or those who aspire to lead because, as we three have all experienced, the above list could be rewritten for negative leaders, whose colleagues:

• *reduce* their individual productivity

• *decrease* engagement among their colleagues

---

3   Tom Rath and Donald O. Clifton, 'The power of praise and recognition', *Gallup Business Journal* (8 July 2004). Available at: http://www.gallup.com/businessjournal/12157/power-praise-recognition.aspx.

- are *less likely* to stay with their organisation

- receive *lower* loyalty and satisfaction scores from customers

But don't take our word for it. Gallup, with its huge database, points out that employees who do not receive praise or recognition are more likely to become 'less productive' and 'disengaged'. Creating a culture of positivity through the strategic use of praise will move centre stage in our journey in this book as we unpick what being the 'decisive element' means in practice in our schools.

Let's just look at one more aspect of the relationship between leadership style and employee engagement and productivity: health and well-being. What can be a minor ailment suddenly seems a lot more draining when coupled with the prospect of working in an environment where you feel undervalued. However, we've also spotted that in the places we've worked that had negative leadership, there was also more genuine illness – some of it a clear result of work related issues.[4] An ex-colleague of ours, who monitors staff absence and has years of historical records for the school in which she works, tells us that she can see clear changing patterns of absence that link directly to the comings and goings of section leaders. On the bigger picture, she also observed that when the leader of the whole organisation changed, with the new head teacher less person centred in their approach, overall absence rates significantly changed for the worse.

---

4   All three of us have direct experience of this: monitoring data has shown that absence linked to work related stress, for example, is seen more frequently in certain areas where there is a negative leadership style.

## More clever stuff

Gallup highlights some of the health-related issues linked to negative bosses: 'boss-induced hypertension could increase the risk of coronary heart disease by one-sixth and the risk of stroke by one-third'. They go on to point out that the health implications, absence rates and lowered engagement means negativity 'cost[s] the US economy between $200 and $300 billion every year in lost productivity alone'.[5]

Now link this to the situation in the classroom. What does this mean for the child who has a snuffly cold or a tummy ache? If there is something at school that they are really looking forward to, they are more likely to make the effort to go to school. If they've got a teacher with whom they find it hard to engage – a teacher who is unlikely to recognise that they are below par and to show appreciation for the fact they have come in, or a teacher who is grumpy, harsh and overly demanding – where is the incentive to go to school? The relationship between school attendance and achievement is well documented and, of course, scrutinised by Ofsted, so the impact of high quality relationships between teachers and kids is crucial.

In all of our discussions about leadership, for 'boss' read 'teacher' and for 'employees' read 'pupils'. It's not hard to make the link and, because we are all human, the way kids feel about their teachers is startlingly similar to how adults feel about their bosses – it's just the vocabulary that is different. After all, teachers are leaders.

In December 2017, Rob Brown compiled a report for the BBC which focused on young people who were opting out of going to school.[6] Clearly,

---

5   Rath and Clifton, 'The power of praise and recognition'.
6   Rob Brown, 'School's dead, it's the same lessons every day' [video], *BBC* (7 December 2017). Available at: http://www.bbc.co.uk/news/av/stories-42254523/school-s-dead-it-s-the-same-lessons-every-day.

there were high levels of disenchantment towards school, and the reasons why they felt there was nothing in it for them were many and varied. However, a number of the respondents pinned the blame fairly and squarely on their teachers. The students expressed dislike and, indeed, distrust of their teachers. They criticised them for teaching the same sort of lessons day in, day out, which became boring for the students, and they accused their teachers of teaching lessons which were irrelevant. Of course, this was a snapshot and there are more sides to the story, but it does highlight the fundamental role that the teacher plays in establishing the value that young people place on their education. In the same way that not getting on with your boss is a prime factor in determining why people leave their employment, so getting on with teachers is critical in determining the extent of young people's engagement with school. When this goes wrong, kids find themselves beyond the reach of the education system, with everything that implies for their future life chances.

# The Decisive Element

With every twist and turn of our national discourse about education, it always comes back to the fact that it is the teacher who is the 'decisive element'. We can debate funding, school structures, school buildings and GCSE grading systems, but all of this is peripheral. The real determinant of success is the relationship between the teacher and the child. As teachers, we all undergo rigorous training either in universities or, increasingly, in schools. We are submerged in theoretical discussions about pedagogy, we are immersed in curriculum content and we are coached in strategies for behaviour management, so all should be well, shouldn't it? Unfortunately, you don't have to scratch the surface too deeply to find whole dimensions where we can still improve and develop our practice.

Chris remembers life as a deputy head in a secondary school where he used to walk the corridors during lesson time. On finding kids who had been told to take time out of class, he would usually enquire where things had gone wrong. Time and again, the response was that it was the teacher's fault – that he or she 'didn't listen'. Unsurprisingly, it often became apparent on investigation that there was more to it than that, but what was interesting was that the trigger response was that the student had a perception of not being valued. There was no quality relationship between that teacher and that child.

After a recent family event Mick gave a lift home to a family friend currently struggling in Year 11, and by way of opening up the conversation he asked how school was going. What followed would have been a perfect précis of this book. It went along these lines: 'I'm doing okay in English. I really like the teacher – she always has time to go through stuff with you if you aren't too sure. We all like sociology – the teacher is really cool. He is funny and makes us want to do it. I'm doing okay in science, which is a surprise because I used to be rubbish at science, but our teacher makes it really interesting. We do different stuff all the time. He encourages me, saying how I can improve so I get it. Maths – oh no, I'm dreading the results of my mocks. The teacher is so boring. She just talks at us as though it was a lecture. She just doesn't get us. Spanish – I nearly fell asleep in yesterday's lesson. Really boring, and she doesn't seem to care about how we do. Just says it is up to us …' So it went on.

Out of the mouths of babes comes the kernel of truth about teachers. As a nation, we have a bipolar view of teachers. On the one hand, we enjoy films such as *Goodbye, Mr. Chips*, *Dead Poets Society* and *School of Rock*, where a much loved teacher, sometimes in difficult circumstances, prevails and makes a difference to the lives of the kids in their care. On the other hand, we have a stereotypical image which informed the creation of Teacher in The Bash Street Kids in the *Beano*: a shouty, naggy, bossy person who tries to make you do things you don't think you can do and probably don't want to do, threatening you with penalty or punishment if you don't. School therefore becomes a never-ending game of cat and mouse, where the kids are as naughty, lazy and uncooperative as they can be without getting 'done'.

Kids are not the only source of informed opinion about teachers. Every adult has been to school and every adult has their tale to tell. This is where brilliant teachers bask in a golden glow of appreciation from former pupils. Gary was recently described as a 'legend' by a former student! He was leading a teacher training session a few days later and asked the attendees to think back to a teacher who had played an inspirational role for them. A woman who was training to become an English teacher recalled her own English teacher who had rowed her and her friends across Windermere, reciting Wordsworth's poetry to them. Mesmerising and unforgettable. Others talked about the teacher who enabled them to grasp things they had found difficult, while yet more spoke of teachers who had been there for them in difficult times and had been a source of strength. Brilliant teachers are never forgotten, and it all comes down to the quality of those relationships. Even if we don't all have daily opportunities to row our children across a lake, we do all have endless scope for creating that magic kingdom in our classrooms where kids feel valued and where they are encouraged to want to do what the teacher wants them to do. Our favourite mantra!

However, the picture is not universal. These were people, by definition, who had been fairly successful at school, gone on to university and were now entering our great profession. Not everyone has such fond recollections. Many people's perceptions of teachers correspond much more closely to the Bash Street Kids version. Comedian Peter Kay provides his own unique insight into his school days, characterising his teachers as 'power mad' and talking about how kids were belittled by having to sit at the 'thick table'.[7] Gary was berated in the pub recently by a guy who described teachers as 'oozing sanctimony'. Mick has had builders in, and over a cup of (generously sugared) tea the conversation turned to what Mick had done for a living. The discussion which ensued was pretty revealing, with a kaleidoscope of stories about where school went wrong for each of them, much of it focused on their teachers. Most sinisterly of all, Chris came across this poem written by Jim Monck, the younger brother of a great friend of his.

### Animal Farm

*Beasts of England you would make us*
*As we cowered in your class,*
*Cornered, while the marks were counted,*
*By the thought we wouldn't pass.*

*Soon or late the day was coming*
*When you'd seize me by the hair,*
*Maddened that I couldn't answer,*
*And impressed with every stare.*

---

7    Peter Kay, *Peter Kay Live: The Tour That Didn't Tour Tour* [DVD] (2011).

*Still I see your swollen forehead,*
*Wildness in a youthful face,*
*Thuggish as your matching curses,*
*Storming straight towards my place.*

*How I cherished my exclusion*
*From your empire on the field!*
*Savage fights to groom your players*
*Were a secret few revealed.*

*But your rage went into hiding,*
*Clutching hands appeared quite tame,*
*Youthful charm was reinstated,*
*On the days the parents came.*

*As they watched with admiration,*
*We alone observed the switch,*
*And we glanced from pig to human,*
*Hardly knowing which was which.*

*For a time we studied Orwell,*
*Learning why his tale was true,*
*I extended what you taught me,*
*Certain we had studied you.*

*Did a scar, repressed and twisted,*
*Groom the hand that came for me?*
*Will a gracious breeze detect it,*
*On a day that sets you free?*

It is a chilling expression of the way a child felt about this teacher and, more tellingly, still feels about this teacher as an adult. The impact teachers have lasts a lifetime. As Dr. Seuss opined, 'A person's a person, no matter how small',[8] and small people grow into big people, but they don't forget. In our profession we make people, forever. Whoever this teacher was certainly made the weather for Jim, and it was the worst sort of weather imaginable. Even if this teacher is banished to the lower reaches of the 1–10 scale for building positive relationships with kids, the experience cannot simply be brushed aside as extreme and therefore exceptional. It provides us with the bottom rung of the ladder on which all the rest of us will climb. Our aim in this book is to extol the virtues of those who ascend to the very highest rung of positive relationships and to analyse and distil how they do it.

As a teacher, the greatest mystery of all is that you often don't know what difference you are making. You are so consumed with the sheer busyness of your classroom that you don't realise how much of an impression a smile, a moment with a child, a word of praise or a listening ear has made. You may not realise it but that child will. In his analysis of resonant leadership, Daniel Goleman reminds us that 'leaders have the power to impact the emotional states of people around them'.[9]

## Here's a challenge for you …

At the end of every day take a moment to be kind to yourself. Think back through your day and calmly, gently remind yourself of moments when you know you made a difference to a child. You were that special teacher!

---

8   Dr. Seuss, *Horton Hears a Who!* (London: HarperCollins, 2012 [1954]), p. 18.
9   Goleman, 'Master the four styles of resonant leadership'.

# Making a Difference, Forever

Brilliant teachers are always sensitive to the impact they have on the kids they teach. They have an awareness that the way they are interacting with their students has implications not just for the here and now, but also for the long term. In each and every interaction, their eyes are fixed on one, and only one, outcome: that next time things should be better not worse. How often have we found ourselves frustrated and exasperated and tempted to administer a good telling off? While it might seem to be natural justice to release some personal bile by giving a young person a piece of our mind, is the result ever that next time the child will be more likely to want to learn or behave better? They may be cowed into temporary compliance, but it will be a fragile truce.

Mick recalls a teacher in one of his first schools who had a reputation as the enforcer of discipline, the hatchet man who would take on the naughty kids. He was a huge bloke and had an imposing presence. He would shout at the kids and threaten them, and in school they would usually conform for fear of another telling off – or at least go through the motions of con-forming. What was interesting was that this teacher cycled to work, and this meant cycling through neighbourhoods in the catchment area. Mick wit-nessed him being on the receiving end of torrents of foul-mouthed abuse on his journey home once the kids were freed from the strictures of the school environment and could say what they really thought.

At the outset of their career every teacher has to answer the question, 'Who am I?' Chris started his career in very challenging schools in South London. He was overwhelmed by the dysfunctional backgrounds of many of the kids, the scale of the disadvantage they would need to overcome and the educational deficit for which he would need to try to compensate. He wobbled around trying to be their friend as well as their teacher, hood-winked into thinking that they needed someone to be nice to them, and that this would be enough to win their favour and respect. But building great relationships is not about being nice all the time. Being their teacher is not the same as being their friend.

In his next school, he started alongside a PE teacher who had been a professional rugby league player. He wouldn't mind Chris saying that he was a stereotypical alpha male: physically big, with a commanding personality and an ego that would move mountains. Chris thought that maybe he should model himself on his colleague. After all, he seemed to command instant respect. Of course, Chris wasn't cut out to be a lookalike for this particular teacher. It worked for the PE teacher but it was never going to work for Chris, so he set out on a different path based on two founding principles: teaching lessons that the kids enjoyed and building brilliant relationships. Chris realised that he needed to be the 'decisive element' for every child he taught.

There is a popular myth that never takes long to surface in radio phone-in programmes or in the press, that things in schools are not as good as they once were. Apparently, there was a golden era when kids behaved perfectly. We are not sure when that was. Chris's father wrote in his diary in 1929, 'We had Divinity today. Everybody just laughed and fooled about,' and this was at Dartmouth where the naval officers of the future were schooled. In the good old days, so goes the myth, the cane was used to enforce discipline. Even when the barbaric notion of beating young children with a stick was outlawed in the 1980s, there was still an understanding that pupils should do as they are told, and there was an assumed respect for the authority of the teacher.

Those days have gone, and not just in schools. Whether you are a police officer, a prison officer or even a member of the emergency services, the days of automatic deference, let alone obedience, are gone. Whether you work for the police force, the prison service or in a school, you will get people to do what you want them to do by the quality of the relationships you have with those in your charge. Building those relationships is immensely complex and can be very time consuming. For teachers, it might be quicker and easier to give the child a good telling off or punish them; quicker and easier but far less effective.

The most successful form of behaviour management is to build robust, quality relationships, but this is immensely complex and can be very time consuming. It is absolutely essential to reach every child, and this requires a rigorous method and systematic record keeping. With the best will in the world, class teachers are extremely busy folk, and due to a major design fault when the world was first set up there are only twenty-four of those time slots we call hours in a day. In the helter-skelter of a school day, certain children demand the attention of the teacher more than others, but brilliant teachers build these great relationships with all their kids.

Our eye is often drawn towards the needy kids or the shining stars, but there are many middle-of-the-roaders who will thrive as a result of having a great relationship with their teacher. Mick watched Chris teach about twenty-five years into his career and at the end of the lesson said to him, 'Do you realise that you give much more attention to the kids on the two tables in the middle of the room at the expense of those on the sides of the room?' Chris thought he was good at this. He had to change his thinking, which proves just how hard it is to reach every child unless you are absolutely systematic.

## Here's another challenge for you …

Pick a particular class and ask yourself, 'Have I given my time and attention to every child in the last couple of lessons?' Go through the class list and check.

How do you build these relationships? It starts with getting to know as much as possible about each child. (We explore this in more detail in Chapter 3.)

What are they into? What TV programmes do they watch? What computer games do they play? Are they into dance, sport, skateboarding or making things? Are they a member of the Scouts, a church group or a drama group? Do they have an unusual interest? (A member of Chris's Year 9 tutor group was a champion sheepdog handler!) Chris's father was a very adept social performer. He had an extraordinary knack of going up to people at family occasions and remembering where their children went to university or what they did for a living. Chris knows it wasn't an accident: he found a little notebook that his father kept with such details meticulously recorded in it.

## A further challenge …

Keep your own version of a little notebook where you record things about each child and even their family. This can be priceless for building relationships; it is so powerful to be able to start a parents' evening conversation by alluding to something which came up at a previous meeting.

Once you begin to assemble these choice pieces of information, you will have a compendium on which to draw. It sends a subliminal message to the child that you care, that you are interested and that they matter to you, which can be deployed in your interactions with them at any time. This can be especially useful when things have gone wrong, when the child is cross or has made a mistake. 'Thank you for telling me about your boxing earlier' or 'I really enjoyed hearing about your rosette at the gymkhana – how did it go on Sunday?' are great ways of defusing the tension and reminding them that they are important to you. Yes, they may have got themselves in a tangle about something, but they are still a good person and there is a way forward. Always separate the behaviour from the child: they may have done something naughty or wrong, but that doesn't make them a bad person. Great relationships are based on the child feeling valued.

## Even more clever stuff

Psychologist Gregg Henriques describes 'relational value' as being the most fundamental of all human motives.[10] He defines it as 'the extent to which one feels valued by important others'; in our case, in our role as the child's teacher. He suggests that relational value may be measured by the amount of attention the child receives, the balance of positive versus negative content of any interaction, the degree of thoughtfulness on the part of the teacher and the willingness of that teacher to put themselves out to help.

What does this look like in practice? First, listen to the child. Remember the cry from kids sent out of class in Chris's school that their teacher doesn't listen. This is not as easy as it seems, not least because Chris knew his colleagues well enough to know that they were the sort of teachers who would listen, but this was not the child's perception. So tell them you want to listen, tell them you are listening, tell them you have listened and, crucially, thank them for having explained their side of things to you. 'Thank you' is such a potent phrase, but it is massively underused as part of the normal dialogue between teachers and kids, and indeed teachers and parents. Saying thank you in itself is a way of saying that you value the child.

As Henriques indicates, every child has a need to be recognised, acknowledged, respected and valued. This will far outweigh material rewards. A young friend of ours regaled all three of us at a recent gathering with an

---

10  Gregg Henriques, 'Relational value: a core human need', *Psychology Today* [blog] (23 June 2012). Available at: https://www.psychologytoday.com/blog/theory-knowledge/201206/relational-value.

account of her recent performance review at work. She had been recommended for promotion and a salary increase but, welcome as that was, the fact that her efforts had been recognised at a particularly difficult time for the company was reward in itself.

# Being Different

As we have seen, when it comes to building positive relationships, the greatest effort is likely to be invested with the kids who are reluctant to engage with school. When having those conversations with kids who have messed up at school, the first hallmark of a brilliant teacher is to dodge the stereotype. Naughty kids are expecting a telling off because that's what happens in The Bash Street Kids. Come at it differently and you will start to be that teacher who becomes really special to them. It will not happen immediately, but over time it will, and once it does you will be that teacher forever.

What sort of teacher do you want to be? Do you want to be the autocratic teacher who barks and shouts in school but has abuse hurled at them once they are outside the sanctuary of the premises? Or do you want to be the sort of teacher who, on a Saturday morning in town, or a couple of years later when you meet them in the pub, or ten years later when you find yourself on the same hospital ward, or thirty years later when you are at the same hotel in Malta (these are all real examples which have happened to us, by the way!), former pupils are pleased to see, as they fondly reminisce about the laughs you had together or how you helped them when they were struggling? The choice is yours.

Simple things can make such a difference. In the early days of his glittering career, Chris taught with a colleague whose favourite ruse with a pupil who had misbehaved was to take them into the departmental office where there was an empty filing cabinet. When the child was least expecting it, she would thump the cabinet, which made an almighty boom and frightened the living daylights out of the secretaries three doors down, never mind the miscreant. Effective in the short term? Maybe. Effective in creating a halcyon glow of happy memories and making that child want to do well, try his or her best and enjoy learning? We don't think so.

Very simple alterations to body language and posture can help. First, come down to the child's level. A teacher towering over a seated child is immediately confrontational. Either sit down or squat by the child (Mick used to sit cross-legged on the carpet!). Once they read the signs that confrontation is the order of the day, the reptilian brain will kick in and they will not listen to the message. Their brain has tripped into fight or flight mode. Second, try to move next to the child, not opposite. Many children find direct eye contact very difficult. This is even more important with people from some cultures who can actually take offence at direct eye contact. There has been a lot of research into the role that eye contact plays in human behaviour, but some children, especially in what they perceive as a confrontational situation, will find it impossible. By sitting side by side, you immediately circumvent this and place the child in an emotional environment where they feel more comfortable, which is more likely to lead to a successful outcome.

When it comes to building relationships with kids who are in trouble for having done something wrong, it is always best to do this in your own time and when the heat has gone out of the moment. Start with a smile and lots of positivity, sit side by side and maybe start with a phrase like, 'Tell me …' so they know you will listen. Always work from the assumption that they are a nice person; yes, they have made a mistake but they are still a good person.

## Another dose of clever stuff

Research by Andrew Meltzoff and Rechele Brooks suggests that within seven hours of birth, babies start to take an interest in their mother's face and have been seen to imitate facial expressions. Between six and eight weeks, babies start to direct their eyes intentionally by looking directly at their caregiver, and by nine to twelve months they follow the eye gaze of the adult.[11]

While such research shows the vital importance of eye contact from the moment of birth, it also helps to explain why children for whom this natural process of development is interrupted find eye contact in subsequent life so hard.

---

11 Andrew N. Meltzoff and Rechele Brooks, 'Eyes wide shut: the importance of eyes in infant gaze following and understanding other minds'. In Ross Flom, Kang Lee and Darwin Muir (eds), *Gaze Following: Its Development and Significance* (Mahwah, NJ: Erlbaum, 2007), pp. 217–241.

## Extra clever stuff

Dr Steve Strand, then of the University of Warwick, used research from the Longitudinal Study of Young People in England in 2004 to show how negatively young people often see their own potential.[12] When asked questions like, 'How good do you think you are at schoolwork?', 'How good do your teachers think you are at schoolwork?' or 'How good or bad do you think you are at maths/English?', children – especially those from lower socio-economic groups and, crucially, boys – often judged themselves very harshly. The way kids see themselves (their academic self-concept) is a crucial factor in determining the likelihood of success at school.

One of the principal obstacles to kids doing well at school is that they talk themselves out of it. They come to believe that they are no good at maths or rubbish at art. With these kids, start the conversation about things at which they excel. Take the focus away from English or maths and look at details they won't even have thought of: have they got lots of friends? Are they reliable? Are they the peacemaker when there is a squabble? Are they kind? Are they thoughtful? Did they have the best smile in the class photo? Was their costume for World Book Day amazing? Build your relationship with them on the basis of what they can do, not what they see themselves as struggling with.

---

12 Steve Strand, keynote presentation to the National Conference on Tackling Boys' Underachievement, Earls Court, London, 17 June 2008.

# Self-compassion

## Clever stuff again!

Dr Kristin Neff is an evangelist for self-compassion and her research has potential applications for us here.[13] She explores the concept of self-esteem which we have already looked at through the prism of Dr Steve Strand's research into academic self-concept. While many children who are not faring well at school, either in terms of behaviour or academic success, will certainly have low self-esteem, self-esteem in itself is an unreliable friend. If we define high self-esteem as feeling above average in something, we have an immediate mathematical problem in so far as we cannot all be above average. Even if we are successful by moving into fixer mode and raising kids' self-esteem, by making them feel better about themselves via psychological mind games (perhaps by improving their academic self-concept), what happens next time they fail in their eyes? They are likely to drop like a stone and will probably feel even more disenchanted.

Neff explores another way forward which will certainly have an application for building relationships with kids for whom school is a struggle – self-compassion. She starts by exploring what compassion looks like: if we see a homeless person on a cold night, the first thing we have to do is notice; then we may want to be kind and generous towards them; and finally we have to acknowledge that we are not going to solve the problem of homelessness overnight. It is a scourge but it is a part of our broken world. Neff concurs with Steve Strand's analysis that we are our own harshest critics. We talk to ourselves in terms we would never use about

---

13  Kristin Neff, 'The space between self-esteem and self-compassion: Kristin Neff at TEDxCentennialParkWomen' [video] (6 February 2016). Available at: https://www.youtube.com/watch?v=IvtZBUSplr4.

other people. We tell ourselves we are no good at writing or science or music, which becomes a self-fulfilling prophecy.

The principles behind self-compassion mirror those of compassion. First, we have to notice – to acknowledge that all is not well. Then we have to be kind and generous to ourselves: we are still good people with lots on the positive side of the balance sheet. We need to be kind and gentle to ourselves, wrapping ourselves emotionally in a bit of serious tender loving care. (This involves the mammalian brain: mammals produce young who are immature and require a great deal of warmth, nutrition and nurture to develop. We must learn to treat ourselves in this way.) Finally, we have to accept that life is not perfect for us and it never will be. None of us has a passport to a wonderful life. We all mess up, we all have things we aren't good at and we all struggle. It's part of being a human being, but it's okay. It is how we are. It doesn't make us a bad person.

Neff's research shows that if we can train ourselves to be emotionally self-compassionate, we will deal with setbacks and subsequent failure with much more resilience than if we go for a temporary but unsustainable lift in self-esteem.

What does this mean for building relationships with kids, particularly the harder to reach kids? Remember, they are hard-wired to expect a telling off from a bossy, naggy teacher. Chris has seen the most reluctant and recalcitrant child change course by using this approach. Start by saying, 'Are you happy with what has happened? Do you think it is solvable?' Almost every time they will say they are not happy and they want things to be better (step 1: notice and acknowledge there is a problem). Then reassure them that they are a good person, that you rate them and value them, even if they have made a mistake, and that you believe that together, with your help, they can move forward (step 2: get them to give themselves some TLC). Finally, explain that sometimes life doesn't work out, it isn't fair and you don't always win (step 3: accept that life isn't perfect; that's how it is). Chris used to talk about how he got a speeding fine: he reckoned it was unfair because he wasn't the only one to break the speed limit. But at the end of the day he had to pay. He had messed up and he had to pay the penalty. Part of growing up is learning that sometimes there are consequences linked to our errors and wrongdoings.

## Another challenge …

When talking to kids who are finding the going tough at school use phrases like:

- I rate you.

- If I were running a business, I would offer you a job because you have got something about you.

- It's okay not to like maths/geography/school …

- It's okay to say, 'That person is not my favourite person,' but it's not okay to behave badly or be rude. We all find ourselves working with people who are not our favourite person. We just have to find a way to make things work.

- This will never be your best subject but I reckon I can help you to be okay.

- You are important to me and to the class. It is never the same when you aren't there. You are probably never going to be top of the class, but I will help you to do the best you can.

- I don't know what you are going to do in life, but you are going to do it very well, once you find something you really like doing. My job is to help you get there.

- You are very good at being on time/turning up looking smart/ getting on with others/hitting deadlines/knowing what to do when others don't/getting on with the person in charge/sticking with it when it's boring/not just starting something well but seeing it through to the end. Obviously things have gone wrong in ... so how can I help?

The 'How can I help?' question is crucial and is a key feature of how brilliant teachers build positive relationships. The chances are that this is not the first time this child has been in trouble. Are you going to be 'just like all the rest' in their eyes, or are you going to be the one who starts to win through? Kids who misbehave are often on a treadmill; this is how they have always behaved. They are children and don't yet know why they behave in this way or how to go about doing things differently. They need your help, and you will earn serious respect from them if you start them on a different road. We recommend that you make some notes for yourself after conversations like this; sometimes it can be useful to share these with the child. This will help you to remember what you said you would do and to check back with the child that you have done it, making it much more likely that next time they will be more inclined to do the right thing.

Mick had to deal with a pupil who had been very badly behaved in one of his lessons. When Mick listened to the child's side of the story, it turned out the pupil, who was 14 at the time, had experienced huge problems at primary school when learning to read. He thought he might be dyslexic. When Mick got in touch with his mum, she said, 'Oh, we've heard all this before. We asked Mrs So-and-So at parents' evening and she said she would look into it, but we've never heard anything more.' The trust was gone and they felt let down – justifiably so.

## Try this

While building relationships with difficult kids, make notes about what you have promised to do and report back to the child and maybe the parents as well.

Parents are potentially your greatest allies in building relationships with children who are not being successful at school. Kids crave approval from their parents. It is very powerful to say to a kid when negotiating your way forward on how they could improve things, 'Would you like me to give your mum/dad/carer/whoever a call to say how well you've done?' And the sooner, the better. With kids who were returning after exclusion, Chris would always commit to phoning the parent after morning break that day, then again at lunchtime and again after school. Remember parents were at school in their time and their perception of teachers may well be the stereotypical Bash Street Kids one too , so it is vital to establish a positive tone and positive engagement. Aim to become the first teacher who really listened, who made the child believe that they could do okay and took the trouble to praise them for doing something right.

Gary tells a story of a very challenging Year 6 pupil who had multiple difficulties in school. Gary taught him for English and this kid did a really good piece of writing one Friday afternoon, so Gary arranged for a text to go home. Next time he saw mum, she was effervescing with enthusiasm. She told him that she had never had any positive communication from school in the six years since her son had started. It would be an exaggeration to say that no one ever had any problems with the lad again, but this one act certainly had a huge impact.

# Using Empathy to Build Relationships

We have alluded to the vital need to listen to kids when building these positive relationships, so we need to give a brief mention to empathy. As we understand it from the brilliant *Sesame Street* characters, empathy is about being able to say, 'I know how you feel.'[14] This can have a liberating effect on a child, and it will be part of the emotionally intelligent teacher's toolkit to be able to see where a child is at and understand their feelings. Chris vividly remembers a child talking to him about what being dyslexic meant to him. He described it as follows: 'All I can see is lots of barbed wire dancing around on the page.' Chris had never understood the problem in these terms before, and it helped him and the child to be able to share that perspective.

A word of warning here though. Children will spot flannel at a hundred paces, and while it can be massively empowering to tell a child that you can now see things from their point of view, it is crucial that you are honest. Mick gave a lot of time to a very needy child who had suffered multiple bereavements, and in these circumstances he felt completely at ease saying, 'I can't possibly imagine how you are feeling.' Sympathy abounded, but empathy? Mick was able to extend his compassion to the child but it would have been fruitless to pretend he knew what it must be like being in that child's shoes.

Between us, we have observed the wider outcomes of negative classroom management, and they can be disastrous for the school but more importantly for the youngsters at the sharp end of a less than empathic approach. We've noticed that in classrooms where there is little positive reward for effort, there is a greater likelihood of lateness and disengagement from the students. In schools where a lack of empathy is pervasive, our experience

---

14  *Sesame Street* and Mark Ruffalo, 'Empathy' [video] (14 October 2011). Available at: https://www.youtube.com/watch?v=9_1Rt1R4xbM.

suggests that there is higher student absence and that minor ailments are more likely to keep them away. The climate must be right.

What we are saying here is that weather gods can work both ways. Teachers can choose to bring in either the sun or the thunder. They can create a world where their pupils bask in a tropical paradise or face the harshness of a Siberian winter. The issue goes beyond learning, beyond whether a youngster can understand fractions or not. It's quite clear that if we link Gallup's research to the world of kids in schools, a stressful classroom can have serious implications. We would also add into this argument that in stressful classrooms, where the emphasis is on firm discipline rather than being reward focused, the kids will be less able to learn.

Our conclusions link with the many pupil voice surveys we've seen and the conversations we've had with youngsters over the years. Kids are rather old fashioned really and prefer teachers who control them and teach them things. This is not the same as being a teacher who commands the class like a regimental sergeant major. Far from it. There is a different way: pupils want teachers who 'get them', teachers who value and respect them, teachers who see the very best in them unconditionally, all the time.

In many respects this is all about time. It's much easier to take a quick route to making the kids do what you want. As we'll illustrate later, that was very much the sort of schooling we all had. There's little to consider when you're being bossy, naggy and shouty – you just do it. Weather god teachers invest the time to build rapport because 'Relationships between staff and students ... are critical in promoting student wellbeing.'[15]

Just recently Gary had a trainee teacher approach him with a problem. The class teacher (her mentor) had been off ill for a few weeks and she

---

15  Public Health England, *Promoting Children and Young People's Emotional Health and Wellbeing: A Whole School and College Approach* (London: Public Health England, 2015). Available at: https://www.gov.uk/government/publications/promoting-children-and-young-peoples-emotional-health-and-wellbeing, p. 9.

had effectively become the class teacher during that time. While it was added pressure and not exactly part of the script, the trainee stepped up and threw herself into the role. However, after a week or so she received a plea from a parent asking her to stay at the school because 'you make the students feel so much happier as you listen to them and they want to work for you'. Similar comments came from other parents and, most importantly, her students said the same thing.

The trainee asked Gary what she should do. She felt guilty about creating a different classroom atmosphere and was concerned that the regular teacher would have difficulties with the students on her return. Obviously, the trainee was not to blame for anything; she was doing exactly the right thing in creating a climate where her students felt valued. But she needed to move on and do the same for her own class when she was qualified. It was the class teacher who needed to do things differently, but that wasn't the trainee's responsibility.

This trainee had all the right instincts for creating a classroom based on a culture of positivity where the kids thrive. But it's not just the kids. Teachers also thrive in the right habitat where the currency of classroom exchanges is a smile, not a snarl; where kids are purposefully engaged and feed back to the teacher about how much they enjoy their lessons. This will extend into relationships with families where parents thank you at the school gate and at parents' evenings. When it's going well, this is all part of the virtuous circle that makes teaching the best job in the world. This book is about ensuring things go well by building positive relationships.

## Top tips

- Teachers are leaders in the classroom.
- Creating a culture of positivity improves outcomes for everyone.

- Make sure that every kid feels valued, and knows it!

- Recognise what the stereotypical teacher is like in kids' eyes – and be different! Know what kind of teacher you want to be.

- Know your kids inside out. Build great relationships day in, day out.

- Listen!

- Use the right language – it makes a difference.

- Make the folks at home your greatest allies.

# Chapter 3
# **Practical Weather Making**

Being a weather god, building great relationships and creating a culture of relentless positivity, whether as a school leader or a class teacher, takes time – a lot of time. Even more intriguing is that every time you start in a new post, a new school or a new class, you pretty much have to begin all over again.

We like the idea presented by Dr Martin Seligman which describes how a positive approach can help young people to flourish and have a major outcome on their well-being. He uses the acronym PERMA:

P – *Positive emotion: high self-esteem and self-worth.*

E – *Engagement: being absorbed in activities that challenge.*

R – *Relationships: positive and meaningful, where you feel people care about you.*

M – *Meaning: feeling that what you are doing is worthwhile and beyond just yourself.*

A – *Achievement: aiming to be the best we can be.*[1]

All of these things, in our view, revolve around the core principle of positive relationships and, according to Seligman, this is a deep part of our development as human beings:

*The important fact that positive relationships always have emotional or engagement or meaning or accomplishment benefits does not mean that relationships are conducted just for the sake of receiving positive emotion or meaning or accomplishment. Rather, so*

---

1 Martin Seligman, *Flourish: A Visionary New Understanding of Happiness and Well-Being – and How to Achieve Them* (London: Nicholas Brealey Publishing, 2011), p. 24.

*basic are positive relationships to the success of Homo sapiens that evolution has bolstered them with the additional support of the other elements in order to make damn sure that we pursue positive relationships.*[2]

It is the teacher's and the leader's responsibility to promote PERMA in the classroom and across their school or area. Seligman has smashed the nail on the head by pointing out to us that we need positive relationships in order to thrive. In the classroom, whatever the age group, it is therefore the responsibility of the teacher (and other support staff) to make that happen.

---

## Beginning the big R

Think of your classes at present. How much do you really know about them?

- Do you know their names?

- Can you put faces to names (we say it this way as you tend to have a list in your register first)?

- Do you know what they all do?

- How many of them can you say you know something personal about?

- Can you make them laugh?

---

Learning names can be a daunting task, but it is the first port of call in creating those positive relationships where people follow you because they

---

2  Seligman, *Flourish*, p. 24.

want to, and not just because they have to; and once the evolution of positive relationships starts to happen, it will ripple through your class and through your colleagues, and it will flood through the school. The mere fact that you, as a leader or teacher, view this as a priority sends out positive signals that you care about the kids and that they mean something to you and the organisation. It doesn't matter if you have ten or thirty in your 'team', using a name matters.

Five hundred names though! Surely, you've got no chance if you are the only RE teacher in the school and teach all of the kids? Even with one hundred it's still a formidable task. We've got a few suggestions that will help you deal with this issue.

The first step is to find out something about each pupil. It can be anything from the football team they support to their hobby on a Saturday. Have they got a bike? Are they an avid watcher of a particular TV show? Do they have a pet? A hobby? A baby in the family? Which computer game do they play? Just find out something to help you create what we call a mini-conversation. Yes, mini. We don't recommend that you sit down for an in-depth discussion on the pros and cons of BMXs over road bikes or the latest *Grand Theft Auto* game. No, that would be a little weird and may well unpick the positive relationship business before you get going.

The second step is mini-conversations, which are little exchanges that simply convey, 'My curriculum leader cares about me and values me' or 'My teacher is bothered about me.' They happen in corridors, in doorways, in the yard, as they arrive and as they leave. It's a simple matter of dropping in a comment about the fact you've found out about them: 'How did you get on with your football on Saturday – it was a bit windy, wasn't it?' This opens up a quick chat which we suggest you don't let go beyond two or three exchanges before you move on. This doesn't need to be a lengthy diatribe about how many forward rolls they did at gymnastics on Saturday. Remember this is a *mini*-conversation.

The mere fact that you are having the conversation signals that you care about them, and the positive relationship builds from there. Mick likens this process to making deposits in an emotional bank account, and it works with both adults and children. Naturally, you develop this process over the course of time as it does take a while to cultivate those relationships. Some folk are more easily influenced in this way than others, so for the individuals who are more of a challenge, you will need to invest extra time and strategies to build the positive link.

The third and final piece of the jigsaw is to make them laugh, although we are not suggesting that you begin your mini-conversations with, 'A man walks into a pub …' or 'Knock, knock …' That would simply make your kids or colleagues think you were odd. Neither are we recommending that you make them laugh hysterically or guffaw their way down the corridor. If that happens, it's not a bad thing, but a smirk, smile or chuckle is more than good enough. Back on the football topic, you might say, 'How did you get on with your game on Saturday – it was a bit windy, wasn't it? I bet you were blown off your feet!' Not a belly full of laughs, but it's light-hearted and may well create a smile. Remember, this is you using your knowledge of what *they* are interested in to create a snappy conversation.

You need to be prepared to invest time in whatever interests them to find out how you might make them smile: 'Is that baby still keeping you awake?' (smile at them knowingly), 'Did you watch *The X Factor* on Saturday night? I couldn't believe Jason was voted off!', 'How's the puppy doing? No more little puddles to deal with, I hope?' and so on. These mini-conversations can run and run and develop further as a rolling soap opera as you learn more about your pupils and new dialogue can be added.

Taking this a step further, think about the most challenging pupils you teach. We bet you know their names! Of course you do. We know exactly why too (we've been there). These pupils need you so much and yet you will often feel that they don't. These individuals need your mini-conversations as much as, if not more than, the rest of your pupils. Some of the kids will intrinsically buy into what you want them to engage with, making the learning process relatively easy; others will come on board quickly if you engage them with positive mini-conversations; and some will need more time and effort but, boy, is it worth investing that time because the rewards will be high.

## Some ideas to get you going

If you had a magic wand and could wave it at your most challenging pupils to engage them in learning, you would, wouldn't you? The bad news is that we don't supply wands, but we do recommend a strategically planned approach with mini-conversations and positivity. Our suggestion is that you choose who, if engaged, could make learning in the classroom easier for all (and your furrowed brow less likely to develop wrinkles). Here's a plan of action you could try:

- Begin as described above, using mini-conversations linked to what you know about the pupils as they arrive at your door.

- Extend this to the corridors, deliberately bumping into them (find out their timetable and ensure you are walking along a route they will take between lessons). Each mini-encounter doesn't have to be conversational – a smile, a hello or a jolly remark will help to build the positive relationship. 'I've got a great lesson lined up for you later.' (Grin and move on.) 'Looking forward to seeing you this afternoon.' (You're not because they were difficult last lesson, but you pile on the positivity.)

- When on duty (hands up all of those who love being on duty?), a much maligned aspect of the teacher's role, you can network and cultivate relationships. Simply breeze past the areas you know your 'targets' spend their time and pass on some positivity.

- In the dining room, just happen to arrive at the lunch queue as they do. There is plenty of opportunity for a mini-conversation.

- Where do they arrive at school and leave? Can you happen to be passing?

- Do they attend a club or play for a team? Show your face.

- As you make progress, can you give them any responsibilities in the classroom? If so, how can you now begin to create opportunities to thank them?

We're not saying this method is foolproof, but we have used this 'saturation' technique over and over again to develop positive relationships with very challenging kids. It may take a week of intense effort or you may have to build it over a longer period, perhaps months. However, once you have built that relationship, it sticks and your challenging pupil can often become your ally in the classroom. We have all enjoyed seeing how well other kids, influenced by a certain pupil, will suddenly become more engaged because their 'leader' is engaged. You may also be surprised by how a youngster you have invested time into will 'pay you back' around the school with offers of help and problem solving. You can't tackle all of your challenging students in one go, so plan who you would like to start with (perhaps not the most difficult), and then as you develop your skills in this area and success grows, invest in another pupil.

Yes, we know what you're thinking: if you had mini-conversations all day you would never get anything else done, and you're right. You need to judge how much of this you need to do (we've suggested that you front-load it with certain individuals), but at the very least, a hello and a smile for every pupil you meet (even better with a name) keeps the illusion going.

Let's now go back to that impossible task of learning the names of five hundred pupils. You don't need to learn names to have positive conversations, but if you do know a child's name it really does help to show them you care. At the end of the Robbie Williams album *Life Thru a Lens* there's a hidden track, 'Dear Sir', a poem by Robbie directed to a teacher who quite clearly didn't understand the value of positive relationships and how important it is for pupils to feel valued. The line, 'The lad called "Thingy" for six whole years', illustrates just how the adult Robbie felt, years later, looking back at a teacher who didn't invest in him. It's so important, but quite tricky if you have a lot of names to learn.

You could spend a few days with name captioned photos and a list of memory techniques, but we will each find the way that suits us best. It's absolutely fine to tell a class that you will work hard to remember all of their names and to apologise if you forget. But avoid the sin committed against Robbie at all costs.

Begin with your main class or tutor group and get your head around their names. You could start with the kids closest to you in the classroom or those you know you need to get into your pocket quickly. In this way, you can give the impression that you remember everyone's name, which of course makes all the pupils in the class feel good. Some people seem naturally good at such feats of recall. Chris and Mick are much better than Gary, who freely admits that he's useless at it unless he makes a real effort. And that is exactly what you must do. These names matter to you, so use whatever trick will help you to commit them to memory. Once you feel you have cracked the immediate 'team', expand a bit further to other classes that you see less frequently. Eventually you will build up your name list, and after a few weeks you will have a wide repertoire.

When it comes to tackling the rest, the key is to target certain individuals using a seating plan, or if you teach a subject like PE or drama, make a list of the groups you set up within the class. It will help if you have a database with photos. Again, who do you need to build those relationships with first? It may be that your target pupil has a best friend, so learn their name too. Are there any other key players in the class that will help to make it buzz? Learn their names too. Do this before the first lesson if you can so that when you see them you will be able to say hello and use their name, which gives a great impression. You may need to glance at your seating plan to help you do this. Over the long term, you are unlikely to remember all of these names but they will build naturally – and if you can also add to your knowledge bank a fact about each child, then even better.

We've said that the first names to learn should be those of your immediate class; however, you may need to take this a step further. Are there any key players you may not teach but who are important to the other pupils? Don't assume this means that you're giving status to the more challenging kids, but do remember that you and the rest of their peers want them on board. Just because you don't have them in your class doesn't mean that you should forget about them. They can have an impact in your classroom simply through their influence over others. Add them to your list. And what about those pupils who have been signalled to you as being difficult; maybe they don't like change, maybe they are a negative influence, maybe they don't like school generally. These pupils all need to be added to your list. Both Mick and Gary have been in this last position and know how crucial it is to target those pupils you need onside to help you build your 'team'.

## It's all in a name

Other great ways to learn names include:

- Glancing at your seating plan so you know the name of a pupil before you speak to them.

- If you read a register out loud, look up, catch the face of the pupil responding and smile.

- Initially with a new class, make stickers or name plates for them that are big enough for you to see.

- Books and folders can have names written in large letters so you can spot them as you move around the class.

- Take a class photo, print a large copy and write their names on it. Keep a copy on your desk, or even on the wall in your classroom, so you can use it as and when necessary.

All three of us are often asked how we remember so many names. We often don't, but running a school requires the school community to believe that you do. By using a combination of some of the techniques above and mini-conversations, you can give the impression that you do know people's names, and therefore pupils and staff are more likely to accept that you care about them. You need to go out of your way to create positive relationships with anyone you feel may pose a threat to your ability so set up a positive team ethos, pupils and staff alike.

We did say it was harder to play the positive game, didn't we? Being a weather god is not an easy option, but it is worthwhile! You must invest time into it but it does pay off. Taking this into a different context, if you are a leader in school nothing is different: you can use the same strategies with the adults with whom you work as you can with the kids. It's all about building positive relationships, so know your team.

# Lessons in Leadership

We three all come from very different backgrounds. Mick was dragged up on a Hull estate – his dad a trawlerman, Gary is from a coal mining background and Chris is from a naval family. None of us followed the traditional family career routes and all of us found our way to becoming leaders in the education business. We each have our own tales to tell, but in this instance it's Chris's that makes the best reading. We've mentioned this in some of our other books, but it is worth considering it again in this context.

Chris's father was a senior naval officer. He captained an aircraft carrier! None of us can actually imagine that – the leader of an incredible piece of machinery, built to both defend our country and to wage war. It had the capability of unleashing a huge destructive force, but of course that couldn't happen without people – the sailors who operated the technology to help the planes take off and land, the navigators, the gunners, the cooks, the radar operators, the boiler men and stokers. Without the humans, the warship was nothing more than a vast lump of benign metal floating around the sea. It took an enormous team of people with more roles that we care to describe to make that ship into an efficient machine. If people did not do their jobs well, the end result could be rather more serious than simply low productivity; it was a matter of life or death. Not the case for your average organisation.

Arguably, the most important of the sailors were the last ones we mentioned – the boiler men and stokers. These were the folk who worked in the bowels of the ship. They shovelled the coal or made sure the oil that fed the boilers flowed to make the steam to power the ship's engines. They made sure those boilers were efficient and produced the power needed to navigate thousands of tons of metal through the water. Without those folk the warship didn't move, and it was exactly this team of men that Chris's father was put in charge of when, at the tender age of 17, he left naval college and took up his first commission as a new officer.

Now, before we go any further, we think it's worth pointing out that the other thing we all have in common is that all of our fathers had a very hands off approach to parenting in our formative years. Mick's dad was at sea for most of the time and Gary's was a typical northern working class man who worked hard all day and spent many nights at the pub. Chris's father, also at sea, perhaps never really got Chris – you would understand why if you met him (Chris, not his father!). He hadn't followed the family tradition of joining the navy and, worse still, he became a teacher – in state education! However, literally on his death bed, Chris's father pointed out an incredible similarity in what they both did for a living: they became leaders.

Drawing him close, Chris's father explained how when he first went to sea, he was taken to one side by the captain and told, 'Henley, I'm putting you in charge of a team of thirty boiler men and stokers.' These men were hard-bitten sailors, who hardly saw the waves or smelled the salt air. Many would have been in the navy for years and some would have been to war. The captain intoned, 'You've got six weeks and you've got to make a first class team out of these men. You need to learn all of their names, some-thing personal about each one of them, you need to know what makes every one of them tick and, above all, you need to be able to make them laugh.' A daunting task for a young man fresh out of training college to become that weather god. Chris had a light bulb moment. He too had his crew, and his job was also to get to know each one of them inside out and to get the best out of each and every one of them.

All of these things are easy to do, with thought and effort, so think of this process as a conveyor belt of relentless and systematic positivity that is part of your everyday to-do list. Make name learning, mini-conversations and positivity part of what you do intuitively every day. It will then become seamless and your ability to engage anyone you want to engage will be far more effective. Viewing it as a tactic to be used sporadically is both perilous and energy sapping, as you will have to think about it consciously rather than simply being aware that it will make a difference in your rela-tionships with your pupils and colleagues.

# Systematic and Relentless

We are now going to add another step to the process: boosting your relationship building with praise. Praise itself is covered in a more theoretical way later in the book, but for now we'd like you to bear with us and trust us when we say that praise is one of the most important tools you can use when developing positive relationships. In fact, we'd also like to convince you that when you praise you should link it to effort, and not talent or getting the right answer. We will explain more about this soon, but for now, as we want you to have the full set of tools to engage your pupils, we will assume you understand this.

We now travel internationally making presentations (it's not as glamorous as you might think) and sometimes our journeys involve long stays in various car parks, otherwise known as the M6 and M1. We have learned from experience that we need positivity to get us through, and one of the most effective approaches we've come up with is to create a 'sweet shop' in the car. It's not complicated, but we'd recommend it to you because while at face value it may sound like an excuse for munching sugary delicacies, we have added an extra spin to it.

The idea arose from a lesson Gary used to teach around the sweet shop scene in Roald Dahl's autobiography of his early life, *Boy*. The passage describes the cornucopia of different treats on offer in the local sweet shop. Gary used to take a selection of different sweets into his class and use them as stimulus for descriptive creative writing. Obviously, the kids left his lesson on a sugar high and probably gave the next teacher a hard time, but that's another story. The twist in our case is a challenge to the person who picks a different type of sweet from the tin (cunningly marked 'The Sweet Shop') in the car. The eater can't put the sweetie in his mouth without starting a new topic of discussion – and it has to be a really juicy one (the topic, not the sweet) so we can pass the time with a good debate and put the world to rights. We recommend it, especially if you like a sweet or two.

No doubt you're wondering what on earth this has to do with praise. Well, in our tin we currently have exactly sixteen different types of sweetie. (Chris counted them specifically, although Gary accused him of using it as an excuse to snaffle one without him being there!) We could easily add further sweets to our tin to boost the choice and temptation, and consequently add to the likelihood of further stimulating discussion.

Now let's turn this around. Imagine you have a 'praise tin' containing all of the different types of praise you use in your daily life – at work, at home and elsewhere. In fact, don't imagine it, write it down on the contents label of this special edition tin. We've added the first one for you.

The secret is to keep adding to your contents list so, like our car sweet shop discussions, you constantly have new ways of delivering praise – except here you are filling the tin as opposed to emptying it. The key is to have a wide range of strategies up your sleeve and to not always use the same ones. Just like a top class sports player, you need to vary your game and keep adding new strategies and options. So, think of the tin you have just inventoried as a piggy bank of praise and continually add to it with new and amazing ideas. Here are a few suggestions to get you going.

# Warm Words

These little beauties are designed to make folk feel good about themselves and what they have done. They can be one-off words such as 'lovely' or whole sentences like, 'That was a really cracking effort.' Weather gods always focus on praising effort, not talent or quality alone. Remember that linking the effort to the outcome has a super positive impact, so you could extend your warm words with something like, 'That was a cracking effort which really made a difference to …'

Brilliant, thank you, fantastic, awesome, amazing, tremendous, love it, wow, great, super, splendid … the list of words you could use is huge, and if you can tailor-make them to your individual situation and the relationship you have developed with the person you are praising, they become even warmer.

Obviously, your words can be passed on in the first person directly to the individual you want to praise. However, why not throw in a couple of twists and praise the person behind their back to someone who will definitely tell them about it. Another strategy, providing you know that the recipient's chest will swell with pride rather than their cheeks blush, is to praise them publicly. This not only passes on the praise but can also send out subliminal messages about the sort of thing you are looking for to others who crave it too.

One important thing to bear in mind is that you need to share out your warm words, not ration them between folk or limit their use. Find reasons to praise all of your class or all of your team – and, yes, we know it's sometimes hard because it's difficult to find praise for someone who is just turning up. (You know, like the person who announces their retirement and someone says, 'I thought they retired years ago!') However, you need to be observant and become like one of those dogs that works in airports sniffing out drugs, except that you have to sniff out reasons to praise. No matter how small, for some folks it can be major step just to be thanked for something. Be systematic about it too, constantly looking at who you have praised but need to top up, who you need to praise as you haven't done so for a while, who you need to get more out of, who you need to get on board, who you need to challenge. Design your warm words to meet the need.

# Written Praise

Some bosses, parents and teachers like to give out gifts and prizes. Gary once observed a lesson where the teacher repeatedly gave out small sweets to those pupils who gave the right answers. Now, that teacher was not only off beam as they only rewarded the right answers (and filled the kids with sugar), but they would not have been able to keep up such a reward strategy for every class for every lesson every year. While the pupils who received the sweets would have loved it while it lasted, they would soon be wondering why the sweeties had dried up, and those who didn't receive a treat would feel they had missed out or weren't good enough.

Similarly, Chris was once given a bottle of champagne and a card by his boss. The champagne was duly quaffed and very nice it was too. However, the card – which thanked him for his effort over the previous term when he'd helped several colleagues through some challenging circumstances – is still in existence and is a great reminder of how impressed his boss was with his work. Chris keeps his mementoes in a box at home, Gary used to stick them to his office wall and look at them if he'd had a hard day and Mick stuck them to his fridge. While there's a lesson here about revisiting the praise you receive to keep your own spirits up, the key message we want to give to you is that written praise can be powerful well into the future.

How often do you send a written note of thanks on a card, in an email, a text, even on a scrap of paper or a sticky note? It takes seconds and makes such a difference. You can leave them on a desk or a bedroom door ('Thanks for tidying your bedroom, Gary') or send them through the post. Email and texts – so simple. Do you send Christmas cards (or cards for other festivals and celebrations) to the people you lead or teach? If not, why not? If you do, make it personal by adding a word of thanks about something they've done. We'll be telling you more about card writing in Chapter 5.

These written warm words are so simple yet so effective, and if you are systematic about it you can play keepy-up with your praise from a distance too. It's the personal touch that matters.

## Challenge …

How many different ways can you find to praise someone without speaking? Why not challenge yourself now and scribble them down here:

# Non-Verbal Praise

We love non-verbal praise techniques for all sorts of reasons, not least because they can be speedy, but mainly because they can also pass under the radar of onlookers and are really useful for those who don't like public praise. Remember, we said that you need to know who you are praising so you can personalise it. With this sort of praise you can add some quirky stuff which lends extra spice and creates a bit of humour. If you haven't attempted them already, we dare you to try these ideas in your context. Oh, and don't think that because your team isn't a class of kids these won't work – everyone likes a bit of fun!

- The whoosh! Wind yourself up and send a double-handed imaginary ball of energy across the room to someone with a whoosh sound. Naturally they have to catch it. You can encourage them to send another whoosh to someone else!

- High one – like a high five, but with a single pinkie!

- Marshmallow clap – imagine clapping but not actually making contact. You've got it!

- Fairy dust sprinkle – scatter some imaginary (because obviously there is real stuff out there) fairy dust on someone's head.

- Seal clap – one for the flamboyant folk out there: clap with the back of your hands and honk/bark like a seal. Lovely if you can get a group of people doing it!

- Twitching thumbs up – just like it says: double thumbs up but with wiggling thumbs.

- Salute – look across a room and salute them. We think the American sloppy version, as opposed to the British ramrod one, works best.

- Round of 'acclaws' – this is complete madness but was suggested to us by a trainee teacher in one of our workshops. Quite simply it's like clapping but using crabby, snapping hands in the air!

If you ever need to give someone an incentive, then predestined praise is for you. Link the praise to a desired action or effort and you're off.

There are many bonus-related pay schemes out there; however, this is not one of those. Nor is it the type of thing whereby a parent might offer a child financial incentives for gaining specific grades. We've not met many people who can change their efforts consistently just for money, and if a target is set that has specific outcome expectations which – despite the person's best effort – are not met, this can have a negative impact on self-esteem and future engagement in work.[3] We don't recommend that praise or rewards are linked to tangible or monetary gain but rather to softer praise incentives. If you have created a positive relationship then merely saying to someone, 'If you work hard at … I will be so impressed with you' or 'The head will be so impressed when I tell them …', will appeal and appears achievable. It is a subtler approach.

If the person works hard at whatever you have talked about, and let's say there are better outcomes, then afterwards there is no reason why you couldn't add a little extra to it. However, the danger of doing this is that you've set up a situation in which someone might expect something similar in the future – and, harking back to our earlier comments, the praise card Chris received was much more long lasting in its effect than the bottle of champagne.

---

3   See Louise Tickle, 'Cash for grades: should parents reward exam results?', *The Guardian* (25 June 2015). Available at: https://www.theguardian.com/education/2015/jun/25/cash-for-grades-should-parents-reward-exam-results.

# Group Praise

Group praise can be very effective in developing a group of folk that you want to bond and work well together. In our experience of leading both adults and children, praising the group for their combined efforts can have several major benefits, especially if you focus your praise on the effort/outcome spectrum. Over the course of our teaching and leadership careers we have often started lessons or meetings by thanking the group for something they have done well through collective effort. In a classroom situation, it might be a class display on *Romeo and Juliet* or with staff how a new rewards policy has been implemented.

The first step in using this kind of praise is to ensure that you have developed a culture of positivity where effort is valued above straight outcome (as covered earlier). This then sets up the opportunity for a leader to be able to thank a group for the efforts they have made, no matter how small or large, and, if applicable, to link it to the outcome they have created. Typically, this can be done in a meeting or group setting, but it can also be accomplished using other means, such as written praise. The key is to reward the group with praise, which we feel benefits those who genuinely put their heart and soul into their work, while adding an incentive (or peer pressure) for those who made a smaller contribution and need to up their game.

Praise of this form can be a great precursor to talking about any areas that you want the group to develop. It illustrates that they can be successful, that they are valued and that you trust them. By linking this directly to another area which needs some improvement, you have already sown the positivity seeds so they are more likely to look at that issue with a 'can do' attitude and set about it with energy. Building on these examples, a teacher could now challenge their class to remember the key words on a display or a leader could ask staff to focus on rewarding a particular type of desirable behaviour displayed by the children.

# Triangulation

Praising an individual can be powerful but by triangulating your praise you can supercharge it. We have used this technique with adults and children and rarely does it fall short. But just as with any praise, you mustn't forget the golden rule of knowing what best suits the context.

It is a bit simpler with youngsters as the triangulation can be much more obvious. Teachers, Scout leaders and coaches can have a major impact on kids with their own praise, but in order to supercharge it you need to add two more 'sources'. Our experience tells us that while teachers have a big influence on their pupils (more so if a child comes from a disadvantaged home), kids are also significantly influenced by their parents and their peers. So, in order to supercharge praise, teachers need to get praise into the pockets of parents and peers.

Gary tells a story about Alice, a reluctant participant in his history class, who in one particular lesson worked harder than usual. Until this point Alice went through the motions and did the minimum to get by. She posed no element of disruption and quietly went about her lessons in order to have an easy life. As a result she was underachieving. She could easily have been heading for a good exam grade, but she was not on course because of her minimal effort and engagement. Gary, who was looking for something to praise, seized on Alice's raised effort one day and awarded her a commendation (a paper certificate for effort). He then started his triangulation plan. After Alice had left the classroom, Gary targeted her best pal in the class and talked about how impressed he was with Alice and her effort, and how it had resulted in some great work. He then sent a text home to Alice's mum saying the same thing. This was all on a Friday afternoon.

The following Monday Gary taught Alice again. As she arrived in the classroom, she called across the room, in front of her peers, 'My mum loved that text you sent her. She gave me £20!' She then turned and grinned at the friend who Gary hoped would tell her that Mr Toward had been praising her behind her back. (Obviously, Gary set up an arrangement with Alice after this whereby he would text home every Friday and they would share the profits. No, not really!) After this it was as if a new dawn had broken. Alice raised her game every lesson, her effort grew and stayed high and she gained the good grades she deserved. Coincidence? Gary very much thinks not.

So, the triangulation process with kids is simple: praise them, send praise to their parents and praise them in front of a valued peer. You then hope the two third parties pass on the praise and, bingo, you have supercharged your praise.

It's a little more complicated, but not impractical, with adults. A word in the ear of the appropriate line manager will almost certainly be passed on, although it is generally not good form to send a note to the elderly parent of an employee! However, opportunities do arise when you meet the wider family of your colleagues, so should an opening arise, use it. It would certainly do no harm – even adults like praise from their parents! Mick once was in conversation with the partner of a colleague at the staff theatre outing and mentioned in passing how much he appreciated all her support in his department during the year. You can bet your bottom dollar it found its way back to her. Even colleagues' children like to be told that their mum or dad is a superhero! The best approach is to find two significant others to utilise in passing on the praise – for example, a friend, a colleague or a senior colleague. It's down to you to make the right choices based on who you think would have the greatest impact.

There are many different ways to praise and build positivity, so be creative. Try to be Mr or Mrs Different: dream up your own unique ways to praise people that will make it special to them and your ability to influence them positively will surely grow. However, here's a challenge for you: fifty-one ways to praise kids you must try before you retire!

1.   Warm words

2.   Stickers

3.   Stamps

4.   Personalised stamps/stickers

5.   High ten

6.   Thank you cards

7.   High five

8.   High five a whole group

9.   High one

10.  The whoosh!

11.  Texts home

12.  Phone calls home

13.  Emails home

14.  Marshmallow clap

15.  Fairy dust sprinkle

16.  Enter into a prize draw

17.  Wear the crown/hat

18.  Look after the cuddly toy

19.  Choose the book

20. Twitching thumbs up

21. Salute

22. Round of 'acclaws'

23. Merits

24. Triangulated

25. Smile

26. Smile with eyes

27. Private warm words

28. Cheesy grin

29. Sing to them

30. Public praise

31. Star of the week

32. Knuckle touch

33. Handshakes

34. Jazz hands

35. Whoop whoop

36. Using sound effects

37. Let them be teacher

38. Sit in the teacher's chair

39. OTT excited words

40. Leave for lunch first

41. Show another teacher their work

42. Trophy

43. Give them a responsibility

44. Badges

45. Clap and honk like a seal

46. Predestined

47. Choose the music of the lesson/day

48. Call the register as a reward

49. In a foreign language

50. In a made-up language

51. Via social media (if your school uses it)

What's for sure is that praise is a crucial arrow in the quiver of any weather god who wants to create a brilliant climate either across their school or in their classroom.

## Top tips

- Think of yourself as an Equity card carrying actor as opposed to a leader. Being at work means you switch on your acting skills; you are the host of your own reality TV show called *Mr/Mrs Positivity Creates Success*. Your persona therefore is always to be on top of your game. You never forget to say hello to a pupil. You never walk down the corridor so focused on how you are going to solve the latest crisis that's hovering over you that you completely ignore the five kids you teach for English or one of your colleagues who you've just passed – and that could be a teacher, a member of the cleaning staff, the estate manager, a lunchtime supervisor, a classroom assistant or any member of the amazing team who make a difference to the pupils. It's crucial that you make eye contact and pass on a smile, at the very least, to all of them. Remember you are creating the weather.

- Remember what we said earlier: your positivity needs to be systematic and relentless. We suggest that every now and again you have a think about who you haven't had positive words with in the last couple of weeks. Some pupils are so quiet and unobtrusive that they can easily blend into the background. You mustn't forget them. Nor should you underestimate the intermittent key players – those who are having a difficult time outside of school. It may be an illness or it may be something social or to do with a relative. Whatever it is, you need to know who they are and ensure that they know you care. Your positivity needs to be relentless because that pat on the back, that thank you, that use of a first name makes so much difference in creating a classroom of pupils who will work for you. And, of course, the same goes for colleagues. Have you let the person in reprographics know recently how much you value what they do? What about the school secretary or bursar? Does every member of your curriculum or year team know how much you appreciate and rate them? It is easy to think that you do this well, but the only way to be certain is to be systematic and relentless. Creating brilliant weather never ends!

And a few shorter tips …

- Get to know names.

- Log information about each child and colleague. Use this in mini-conversations to build positive relationships.

- Make a point of letting them know regularly that they matter to you and that you value them.

- Encourage them with your infinite positivity and make them believe they can be the best version of themselves possible.

# Chapter 4
# Praise and Positivity

The verb 'praise' is defined by the Cambridge Dictionary as 'to express admiration or approval of the achievements or characteristics of a person or thing'.[1] It's very easy to be narrow minded and restrict praise to something that is simply said. However, our view is that praise can be much more than this and should only be limited by the power of the praise giver's imagination. If you want to change the weather in your class or as a school leader, then praise is fundamental to shifting people's perception of themselves for the better.

Praise, in its most common sense, is a direct communication from one person to another, and if carried out in the right way, it can have an amazing effect. Whether it is something that is said face to face, on the phone, via text, email or social media, the fact that someone says something positive about what you have done (or do) is very powerful.

There's nothing like a metaphorical pat on the back to raise the spirits, although some interesting research suggests that while praise gives us a positive feeling, it's actually feeling fully engaged in our work (or our lives) that releases the pleasure chemical, dopamine.[2] However, from our perspective, looking back at over a hundred years of combined leadership of pupils and adults in large organisations, we rationalise this by regarding praise as being much more than words.

It seems to us that if you are working or living in an environment where you feel valued and fulfilled – whether it be a factory, a school, an office or

---

1   See https://dictionary.cambridge.org/dictionary/english/praise.
2   Bruna Martinuzzi, 'What our brains look like on praise and criticism', *American Express Open Forum* (1 August 2014). Available at: https://www.americanexpress.com/us/small-business/openforum/articles/what-our-brains-look-like-on-praise-and-criticism/.

a home – you are going to be happier and feel more successful. Weather gods create the right climate for everyone to thrive. In fact, research suggests (as we will show a bit later) that people who work in an organisation that focuses on negatives or where their boss berates them regularly are much more likely to reduce their commitment and the quality of their performance. Clearly, working or living in a positive environment will produce better outcomes than a negative one.

This form of flattery stretches from very private words to very public praise; some people crave both and many actively seem to need it to survive. Arguably, the most public praise fest in the world occurs every spring with over 30 million people worldwide typically watching the lavish Oscars ceremony. It's a huge event, costing US$44 million in 2017, with spectacular sets, music from top performers and a high profile master of ceremonies.[3] The venue is packed with nominees, Hollywood 'royalty', media representatives and fans.

All of the Oscar nominees have a chance of winning in one of the twenty-four categories. Just to be nominated is a great honour so getting on to that shortlist is already high praise for the contenders: it means that the world is being told how talented you are or how good your movie is. Those nominees who don't win in their category will go on to use the 'shortlisted for' tag in future works to enhance their reputation. However, landing the award is at another level. Many winners have been moved to tears (although we'd like to point out that most of these were actors) or rendered speechless by the situation. On winning the best actress award

3   See Michael O'Connell, 'TV ratings: Oscars drop to 32.9m viewers, telecast takes a bigger hit with younger set', *Hollywood Reporter* (27 February 2017). Available at: https://www.hollywoodreporter.com/live-feed/tv-ratings-oscars-drop-again-early-numbers-980854; Andrew Pulver, 'Costing the Oscars: and your bill for the evening is … $44m', *The Guardian* (26 February 2017). Available at: https://www.theguardian.com/film/2017/feb/25/oscars-2017-how-much-does-hollywood-biggest-party-cost-earn.

for *Erin Brockovich* in 2001, Julia Roberts summed up her huge desire for the praise bestowed upon her with the comment, 'I love it up here!'[4]

We're not suggesting that the kids in your class will stand up after you have awarded them a merit for their effort in handwriting and make an acceptance speech to the class thanking everyone from their best friend Sanjeev to their Auntie Sheilagh who takes them to swimming on a Tuesday. But what we do know from our experience is that kids will grasp hold of those little rewards just as readily as a Hollywood star would an Oscar statuette, and the feelings of self-worth can be just as powerful and will change the classroom climate for the better.

# Creating the Feel-Good Factor

As we saw in the last chapter, praise is not limited to words. Weather gods find many other ways, from the obvious written notes and gifts to signs and symbols. Furthermore, praise does not always need to be explicit. The mere suggestion of approval can be accepted as positive recognition. In fact, we would argue that the nature of the act of praise itself (or the words used) can be relatively unimportant. The fact that someone *feels* praised is what makes praise work, which is exactly the focus of Maya Angelou's famous maxim where she makes how *we feel* the central issue.

Taking this one step further, we are going to put it to you that praise can exist without specific direction or content. We believe that praise can be a feeling that is gained from a positive interaction with another person which makes one or both feel good about themselves. We also think that this almost subliminal praise can exist within a culture of positivity in, say, an organisation or a family where, by the very nature of the interactions and

---

4    Julie Kosin, 'The 20 most memorable Oscar speeches given by women', *Harper's Bazaar* (28 February 2016). Available at: https://www.harpersbazaar.com/culture/film-tv/a10057/best-oscar-speeches-given-by-women/.

environment, the individuals absorb the warm glow that indicates they are valued and respected. They *believe* they are praiseworthy.

## Clever stuff

In this chapter, we stress our strongly held belief that people work better and are more productive and successful in a positive culture in which they are praised and so feel valued, encouraged, engaged and happy. This holds true for staff and pupils. But is there any evidence to support this?

To help answer this question, let us signpost you to a fascinating and persuasive article by Emma Seppala and Kim Cameron.[5] They argue that praise and positivity work, and that this can be proved by a growing body of research evidence on a series of workplace problems. For example:

+ Job stress leads to deleterious impacts on workers' health, leading to high healthcare costs: 'Stress-producing bosses are literally bad for the heart.'

+ Highly pressured environments lead to high worker disengagement: 'Engagement in work – which is associated with feeling valued, secure, supported and respected – is generally negatively associated with a high-stress, cut-throat culture.'

+ High staff turnover and lack of loyalty: 'workplace stress leads to an increase of almost 50% in voluntary turnover'.

+ Worker preference for a positive work environment over company perks: 'Wellbeing comes from one place, and one place only – a positive culture.'

---

5    Emma Seppala and Kim Cameron, 'Proof that positive work cultures are more productive', *Harvard Business Review* (1 December 2015). Available at: https://hbr.org/2015/12/proof-that-positive-work-cultures-are-more-productive.

Their conclusions lead them to identify four steps which leaders can employ to cultivate a caring, positive and healthy workplace culture. These are:

+ *Foster social connections between workers.*

+ *Show empathy.*

+ *Go out of your way to help.*

+ *Encourage people to talk to you – especially about their problems.*

In the autumn of 2015, England were dumped out of the Rugby World Cup on their own turf after a humiliating defeat to Australia. *The Guardian* described the English team as 'shambolic'[6] and, without a doubt, the English rugby union community was shocked at the manner of their departure. England seemed like a broken team and the manner of the loss signalled the end for their coach, Stuart Lancaster. Fast forward six months to the Stade de France in Paris and a score line of France 21–31 England – a win that gave England the Grand Slam having also beaten Italy, Scotland, Wales and Ireland in the Six Nations Championship. Six months after disaster, England couldn't stop winning and what followed was even more incredible: a tour of Australia where they won every test match, an autumn series where they beat all comers and a run in the 2017 Six Nations where they won every game except the final one which they lost to Ireland. Nevertheless, they still won the competition and equalled the New Zealand All Blacks' record of winning eighteen consecutive games.

What changed? While there were new players in the squad, predominantly this was the same team that was so poor eighteen months earlier. One of

---

6   Dan Lucas, 'England v Australia: Rugby World Cup 2015 – as it happened', *The Guardian* (3 October 2015). Available at: https://www.theguardian.com/sport/live/2015/oct/03/england-australia-rugby-world-cup-2015-live.

the players to particularly stand out was Billy Vunipola, and he gives us an insight into what might be the reason: 'I respond more to the love and compassion he [Jones, the new coach] shows the boys, me especially … I don't need someone to shout at me. He has just filled me with confidence.'[7] If you take Billy's perspective, then it seems that a transformational change in culture and climate had occurred, brought on by a different, possibly more positive, leadership style from Eddie Jones, meaning the players feel valued and reassured, resulting in obvious success. Eddie Jones was the weather god the team needed.

As we move forward, we are going to talk about praise and positivity in the same context. How might teachers lead their pupils to get the best out of them? We'll look at some science from super clever folk and link it with our combined experience, and hopefully you'll find some things that will help you to become a weather god in your classroom.

# What Do I Praise People For?

Let's take a breather. Here's a pub quiz question for you: who is most often credited with inventing the light bulb? The phonograph? The motion picture camera? The magnetic iron ore separator? And many more things. The same man who in his lifetime held a record breaking 1,093 patents (either on his own or with other inventors).

Did you get it? It's Thomas Edison. Pure genius? Brilliance at work? Well, not entirely; it depends on where you think genius comes from.

---

7   Gavin Mairs, 'Six Nations 2016: England's Billy Vunipola thriving on Eddie Jones' "love and compassion" ', *The Telegraph* (8 February 2016). Available at: http://www.telegraph.co.uk/sport/rugbyunion/international/england/12147326/Six-Nations-2016-Englands-Billy-Vunipola-thriving-on-Eddie-Jones-love-and-compassion.html.

Thomas Edison, the prolific inventor who tested thousands of theories and prototypes before coming up with the light bulb,[8] reckoned that 'Genius is one percent inspiration and ninety-nine percent perspiration.' Many similar sentiments have been repeated by a range of different people throughout history. We have even heard the great icon of British footie, Golden Balls himself, David Beckham express a similar sentiment on the telly about his own not inconsiderable success on the pitch.

For Edison, his genius lay not in some god given talent but in his relentless effort, dedication and doggedness to never give up. Things did not always come to him quickly or easily. This gives rise to a fascinating question: are we born with innate talents and fixed intelligence which we choose to develop, or not, as the case may be? Bear with us here – we are not heading off on a tangent. We're heading for a rich vein of thinking that you can link to your praising practice. If the answer to that question is no, does that mean we can develop and grow our abilities, if we are operating in the right kind of conducive environment and frame of mind?

Regularly praising someone for having great ability or talent can't hurt, can it? If we praise a child for their ability when they do well that will make them feel clever and that clever feeling will give them more motivation to learn – it's common sense, right? Well, up to a point, but educational research in the United States and the UK challenges this viewpoint. This is tricky stuff and centres on the relative merits of praising ability and the person rather than effort and process. This is not an argument about whether we should praise, but rather *how* we praise. If Edison was right, and we think he was, then our praise will be more effective in terms of long term success and improvement if we use it to encourage and motivate effort, dedication and perseverance.

Our own combined experience at the chalkface tells us that children (in school or at home) who are regularly praised for their personal ability ('Well

---

8    Although there is much debate about him being the first.

done – you're a star', 'High five for talent', 'You're great!') can become more cautious as they get older. Gary remembers one particular girl who was in his tutor group. She was good at art, a natural talent, but what happened to her illustrated how talent alone is not enough and how the wrong praise can hinder development. At parents' evenings over the years, it became quite clear that her parents thought she was very gifted and the praise they used was mainly around her ability. In particular, Gary remembers that she began to draw Disney characters and this carried on for months. In fact, whenever he saw her doodling, it was the same characters. She was very good at it. At a later parents' evening, her parents praised how well she could draw Disney characters, again reinforcing this talent. Choosing art as an exam subject seemed obvious and, of course, her parents expected her to do well. However, her early results were not good. Her art teacher could not get her to move away from cartoon characters. She had become so comfortable knowing that her drawings in this style were good that she could not take risks by experimenting in other ways.

Imagine the picture at home as you listen to your daughter practising a recently learned piece on her guitar. It feels natural and easy to praise her for being a great guitarist: 'Awesome, Jen. You're amazing. You've got talent and you're going to be a rock star!' Sounds okay, doesn't it? We think not. It's the same as with the Disney cartoons. If your praise is constantly about the personal talents she was born with, Jen may well get stuck in a vacuum of personal talent glue. She may become so comfortable in her knowledge that she has this talent that she feels no need to challenge herself further.

We've seen this first-hand over and over again, both in educational settings and with parents. When the praise is focused purely on talent, it eliminates the need for further development and sucks out risk taking and creativity. A fixed mindset is created. The most common scenario we have seen has been with sport, and in particular football, where naturally gifted kids who rock up at school and gain a reputation for being good with the ball have parents who desperately want them to be professional footballers and praise them constantly using talent as the main focus. In our experience, these kids tend to do brilliantly at school and in local teams, but they are often lazy in training, not bothering to turn up at times. They are still so good that they outshine their peers, so teachers and local coaches still play them in their teams. But their less obviously talented teammates often overtake them and may go on to have a professional career, while the more naturally talented player never goes beyond a good standard of local football.

Jumping back to Jen and her guitar, a better approach with praise might be, 'That's awesome, Jen. You've improved again after that hard graft last week, and if you keep working that hard on your pinched harmonics you'll be rocking!' By praising a child's effort or the processes they've used to learn, weather gods open up the possibility (and, crucially, the belief) that they can improve and develop their ability or talent. If your praise overlooks constant practising and a fierce determination to succeed, even in the face of a super challenge, then our experience in schools and with our own kids (also backed up by research, as we'll soon see) has shown us that we run into two bits of risky business:

1. As they get older children can become risk averse. They can be reluctant and hesitant about having a go at that new and more difficult piece of music for fear of failure and the loss of your praise and approval. Like 'praise junkies' they will stick to what they know they can do and not extend themselves. It's safer not to try something hard and risk suffering a setback in case they miss out on the praise hit which they have grown to expect and love: 'I'm good at this – why try something harder and look daft when I can't do it. Stick to what I know I'm good at.' It's worth asking yourself if you recognise this in your own kids if you are a parent, or in your pupils.

2. By constantly banging on about their special talents and god given abilities, we run the very real risk of telling our children that their future is fixed because their intelligence or ability is something which

was given to them (or not!) and fixed (or not!) at birth. If they can only do what their innate talent lets them do, it's therefore pointless to try something new that is really difficult: 'That's too hard for me – I'm good but not *that* good.' They just don't think they have the ability, so there is no point trying.

In our experience of working in schools in the UK, this is a particular issue with boys, especially teenage boys, and especially white working class boys. This might explain why white working class boys underperform in almost every measure in schools, and at every age, compared to girls and to boys from other, more affluent socio-economic backgrounds, and why the country's lowest school achievers are white working class boys.[9] Food for thought? Mick and Gary have worked in several schools dominated by white working class families – euphemistically referred to as 'challenging schools' – where, sadly, this is often the case.

*White British FSM (Free School Meals) boys achieve the lowest grades at GCSE of any main ethnic group, with just 24% achieving 5 A\*–C grades inc. English and maths. They have now been either the lowest or second lowest performing ethnic group every year for a decade.*[10]

Mick remembers working with one white British boy who worked hard, achieved great results, behaved well and did his parents proud. He was in conversation with Mick who was his form tutor and history GCSE teacher at that time. They were discussing his future after school. The boy said he would like to work with kids in a school and asked how he could get into teaching assistant jobs. Now, being a teaching assistant in a school is a brilliant and incredibly worthwhile role, but this boy had the potential to go to university and become a history teacher. The only issue was, as he

---

9   See https://www.suttontrust.com/newsarchive/white-working-class-boys-have-lowest-gcse-grades-as-disadvantaged-bangladeshi-african-and-chinese-pupils-show-dramatically-improved-results/.

10  See https://www.suttontrust.com/research-paper/class-differences-ethnicity-and-disadvantage/.

told Mick, 'Yeah, that's all well and good – I'd love to be a teacher. But that's not for kids like me in families like mine. None of us have ever gone to uni.' He would have made a great teaching assistant, but because he began to realise that he could choose something else, he did in fact go to university, graduated in history and is now a successful teacher who finds the job immensely rewarding. Too many boys like him from families like his don't believe that they are born with talent and so think their future is strictly limited. And all too often they don't fulfil their potential.

# A Growth Mindset

If you find it hard to accept the idea that some kids grow up believing there is a glass ceiling on their aspirations, then take a little time to think about this situation which Chris, Gary and Mick have seen many times as teachers. Imagine the scenario: as head of Year 9 you have a group of thirty teenage boys engaged in a conversation about their future studies and GCSE option choices. You ask them if they think they can take up and learn some new challenging stuff such as higher level maths, physics or French. Trust us, you will get a lot of answers along the lines of, 'No, I'm not good at that,' 'It's too hard for me' or 'I can't do French.' Then ask the exact same group if they are going to learn to drive. We would lay a small wager that the overwhelming majority will look at you as if that was a pretty daft question: 'Doh! Of course we will – everyone does.'

You will struggle to find a teenager who doesn't feel pretty sure that they will be able to master one of the most complex and challenging skills out there. Why? Because they believe they can drive because they want to drive and, crucially, because even if they fail the test a couple of times, they know that if they keep practising then they will get there and pass eventually. In the driving context, they simply don't believe that their ability is fixed – they can grow it. However, in French, physics, maths or other challenging subjects in school, their ability only goes so far – it's fixed.

Research by people like Carol Dweck would call this having a 'fixed mind-set' or 'growth mindset' about what they can learn.

Although we said that it was best not to praise for talent, we are not some kind of anti-talent police, and we are of the view that success and talent can be grown and developed. However, weather gods think it is far more productive to praise a young person for traits they have the power to change, such as effort, practice, process and determination. By investing time and developing these qualities, they can succeed, develop and grow.

Let's take a couple of interesting examples of successful people who exemplify this view:

> *If people knew how hard I had to work to gain my mastery it would not seem so wonderful after all.*
> **Attributed to Michelangelo**
>
> *I don't believe in magic. I believe in hard work.*
> **Richie McCaw, New Zealand All Blacks captain**

We will all remember the praise and feedback we got from teachers and other adults in school and how it came in many forms – you might even be as odd as Mick who still has loads of his exercise books from secondary school stashed in his loft! The teacher might simply have patted you on the back or praised you face to face. Perhaps they did it in writing when they marked a piece of your work. Written praise and feedback follow the same rules and patterns as verbal praise as far as effort and ability are concerned.

This leads nicely to an observation from our professional experience in secondary schools about a pretty standard practice for marking work (which readers may well recognise). A grade ranks the standard of the work, alongside written feedback to explain why the work was graded in the way it was, what has gone well and also what the child might do to improve their work in the future. All too often the response from the child is to look straight at the grade, make an instant judgement on whether it's telling them that they have ability or not, and virtually ignore the written praise and developmental feedback. Another signal that by praising ability we risk limiting and closing down improvement.

A great deal of brilliant work is currently going on in schools, with all ages, to develop marking and assessment systems which avoid the dilemma of assessing and praising work for its standard versus assessing and praising work for improvement. Teachers across the country are wrestling with the problem of trying to get the balance right between the two.

## Lots of clever stuff

Carol Dweck is a leader in education theory in the United States and a world renowned psychologist at Stanford University. Along with her colleague, Claudia Mueller, Dweck conducted detailed research with groups of children to test out their thoughts on the impact of praise for intelligence and praise for effort. Their findings challenge what seems to be common sense thinking: that by telling a kid they are really smart, they will feel great about themselves, pump up their chest and fly off into the next even greater challenge full of confidence and determination. That's not what Dweck found out. She sums it up like this: 'Praise for ability is commonly considered to have beneficial effects on motivation. Contrary to this popular belief, six studies demonstrated that praise for intelligence had more negative consequences for students' achievement motivation than praise for effort.'[11]

11 Claudia M. Mueller and Carol S. Dweck, 'Praise for intelligence can undermine children's motivation and performance', *Journal of Personality and Social Psychology* 75(1) (1998): 33–52 at 33.

In these experiments with fifth graders (primary, Key Stage 2 or Year 6 in the UK), Dweck and Mueller found that kids who were praised for being clever and intelligent cared more about continuing to look clever rather than improving and getting better. If they didn't do as well as their cleverness meant they should, they tended to give up, not persevere and improve. The opposite was true for kids praised for effort.

Now for the really interesting bit. We mentioned growth and fixed mindsets earlier, so it's time to delve into this a bit more. Dweck developed her research about the effects of praise for intelligence or effort into a broader theory on mindsets. The crucial idea is that intelligence and abilities are not fixed, but instead, given the right conditions (including careful use of praise), can be developed and grown. Dweck calls this the 'growth mindset theory'.

She explains why praising intelligence and ability doesn't always foster self-esteem and lead to achievement, but can actually jeopardise success. There is evidence that praise delivered using personal terms about a child's (or colleague's) abilities or talents ('You are clever and really talented at that') can be far less effective at securing improved outcomes than process terms about their effort and resilience ('You worked hard and didn't give up when you came across a problem'). For those readers who wish to explore this work on mindsets more deeply, we would point you to Carol Dweck's book, *Mindset: The New Psychology of Success*.[12] It is very important to note here that Dweck is clear that the strategies used to develop a growth mindset in our kids (including praise for effort and process) work just as well for adults.

> I had a duty to be the best I could be, to see how far I could get. You will always regret it if you don't push yourself.
>
> Martina Navratilova[13]

Dweck describes a fascinating intervention that would teach kids a growth mindset.[14] We think this is brilliant stuff and illustrates the point

---

12 Carol S. Dweck, *Mindset: The New Psychology of Success* (New York: Random House, 2006).

13 Quoted in Matthew Syed, *The Greatest: What Sport Teaches Us About Achieving Success* (London: John Murray, 2017), p. 226.

14 Carol S. Dweck, 'The perils and promises of praise', *Educational Leadership* 65(2) (2007): 34–39. Available at: http://www.ascd.org/publications/educational-leadership/oct07/vol65/num02/The-Perils-and-Promises-of-Praise.aspx.

of thinking about mindsets really well. She was working with seventh graders in junior high schools in New York (secondary, Key Stage 3 or Year 8 in the UK). The kids in the intervention had just made the transition to junior high school, which can be a time when students find school a real challenge and grades can plummet. She developed an eight session workshop in which the control group and the intervention group learned study skills, time management techniques and memory strategies.

The intervention group also learned about their brains and what you can do to grow your intelligence. They learned that the brain is like a muscle that needs regular use and exercise to stretch and grow. They learned that every time they tried really hard and learned something new and challenging, their brain made new neural connections. They learned about medical science discoveries which show brain plasticity, meaning that our brains are not rigid structures – they can change and evolve depending on how we exercise and use them. This proved to be dynamite to these seventh graders. Dweck reports some of the more amazing personal comments – one of the most unruly boys said, 'You mean I don't have to be dumb?'

Their results improved as well. There had been a general steep decline in maths grades among the kids as they entered junior high school. After the intervention, this decline continued in the control group but improved in the intervention group. Dweck was so pleased with the outcomes that she went on to develop an interactive computer based version of the intervention called Brainology and trialled it with kids in twenty more schools in New York. From one kid came the comment, 'If you do not give up and you keep studying, you can find your way through', while another said she could, 'picture the neurons growing bigger as they make more connections.'

There are two caveats from the research into children's motivation: first, boys tend to be more comfortable with ability praise and girls with effort praise. Second, whereas younger children are inclined to see ability and effort working together and derive their self-worth from both, as children get older their self-worth is derived more from ability than effort.[15] For older children, the research suggests that we should avoid praising them for things that come easily to them as they may view such praise as just another way of saying we think they are pretty low ability: 'You're praising me for such a simple thing because you think that's all I'm capable of.'

The last word on this goes to Carol Dweck: 'Our research shows that educators cannot hand students confidence on a silver platter by praising their intelligence. Instead, we can help them gain the tools they need to maintain their confidence in learning by keeping them focused on the *process* of learning.'[16]

Dweck is confident that praise as a strategy to develop a growth mindset works equally for adults (work colleagues, friends and family) as for

---

15  See Jennifer Henderlong and Mark R. Lepper, 'The effects of praise on children's intrinsic motivation: a review and synthesis', *Psychological Bulletin* 128(5) (2002): 774–795.

16  Dweck, 'The perils and promises of praise'.

children. In an interview with Sarah Green in the *Harvard Business Review*, she is clear that evidence about praise with children in schools fits just as well for adults in the business and corporate world. The message is the same: praising effort and process helps to develop a growth mindset, while praising the person and inbuilt talent can lead to a fixed mindset. Dweck explains: 'People who are praised for talent now worry about doing the next thing, about taking on the hard task, and not looking talented, tarnishing that reputation for brilliance. So instead, they'll stick to their comfort zone and get really defensive when they hit setbacks.'[17]

That's great in telling us what not to praise, but it begs the question, what *do* we praise with our work colleagues? Dweck says: 'The effort, the strategies, the doggedness and persistence, the grit people show, the resilience that they show in the face of obstacles, that bouncing back when things go wrong and knowing what to try next.'[18]

Can you see the impact of praising for ability or effort and person or process when applied to the local Sunday league men's football team that you coach? Is it all about the innate ability of the current players in the squad, or can they be developed and improved by the right coach who praises and encourages hard work, training, relentless skill drills and teamwork? Would you take notice of the view of arguably one of the best footballers in the world, Lionel Messi: 'I'm lucky to be part of a team who help make me look good and they deserve as much of the credit for my success as I do for the hard work we have all put in on the training ground'?[19]

---

17  Ibid.
18  Sarah Green, 'The right mindset for success' [interview with Carol Dweck], *Harvard Business Review* (12 January 2012). Available at: https://hbr.org/2012/01/the-right-mindset-for-success.
19  *Attitude*, 'Sporting heroes month: Lionel Messi' (28 May 2015). Available at: https://attitude.co.uk/article/6721/sporting-heroes-month-lionel-messi/.

What about the adults in the team you lead at school – key members of your senior leadership team, your department or year team? Weather gods think the messages are the same: praise for success is important but praise for the process (involving effort, resilience, practice, teamwork and persistence) can lead to continuing success. It's not all about intrinsic ability; if at first you don't succeed, try again or try doing it differently.

# Praising for Effort

Before we finish, here's something you might find odd. We also recommend that you praise when folks get it wrong! We've had the pleasure of watching so many fantastic teachers teach that we've lost count. The very best make use of this technique because they want to encourage their pupils to take risks: 'Praising what people do is more effective at creating improvement than when praise is just about the result. This can be used to praise hard work even if there was little success, and which hence leads to increased effort towards a later success.'[20] We're saying that praising effort is king.

Nearly every class has at least one super eager beaver child who will have his or her hand up like a rocket, answering the teacher's question before it has been fully asked. Quite often the answer is way off the mark and frequently also quite bizarre. Gary once heard this in a Year 1 class:

*Teacher: So, what do we get if we add 2 to another …*

*Pupil (hand shooting up and blurting out): A giraffe!*

How do we deal with this? We'll tell you in a second, but before that we'll explore the time Gary saw how it shouldn't be done in gory detail. A local minister was visiting Gary's school years ago and set about delivering an

20  See http://changingminds.org/explanations/motivation/praise.htm.

assembly to a large group of around 200 Year 6 pupils. At one point he asked his audience a question and, quick as a flash, a lovely lad in the front row shot his hand up and twitched it frantically to gain the man's attention. Having been ensnared, he looked at the boy and gesticulated for the answer, which was proudly shouted out and as equally off beam as the aforementioned 'giraffe' answer. The minister, rather taken aback, barked 'No!' at the boy and moved on, leaving the youngster wilting in front of his peers. His efforts quashed. His excitement ripped from him. The likelihood of him ever answering a question in assembly again? Nil!

Is there a better way? In fact, the teacher with the 'giraffe' child absolutely nailed it. The exchanged continued:

*Teacher: Thanks for that, Charlie. It's not the answer I was looking for but I love your answer. Folks, thanks to Charlie we can now eliminate 'giraffe' from the answer of adding 2 and 2, so what do we think it is?*

Of course, Charlie was rewarded for her effort by a superb bit of quick thinking by her teacher and consequently would readily contribute in class again. By using praise and encouragement based on effort when dealing with the wrong answer ('I love your answer. It's not quite what I'm looking for but thank you for trying'), weather gods encourage participation and risk taking. Not only that, they begin to develop bouncebackability too.

Praise is a vital tool in developing a culture of positivity, which in turn leads to better outcomes for the kids. However, use praise unthinkingly at your peril: steer clear of praising talent, getting things right or just being good at something, and instead link your praise to effort and outcome. This will help to create a 'can do' ethos in your classroom and school, helping to unlock kids' creativity and resilience.

## Top tips

- Praise can change the weather and transform people positively.

- Praise exists as a natural part of a culture of positivity.

- Praise for effort above talent.

- Link the effort to outcomes or gains made.

- Praise for process can unlock creativity and risk taking.

- Praise for effort will help kids and staff bounce back when they fail.

# Chapter 5
# Getting the Most Out of Praise

We have established that one of the key instruments for building positive relationships is the use of praise. Great leaders, like great teachers, are great users of praise.

It is a universal truth that praise is a good thing. On the balance scales of life, it is definitely on the plus side, along with chocolate, Father Christmas and Julie Andrews's favourite things in the *Sound of Music*.[1] Imagine a life without any of those. Ugh. So, what does great praise look like?

The baseline here is that some people have a natural disposition to want to make others feel good (although we are firm believers that we can all learn how to improve our use of praise as a strategic tool). These are the sunshine people who it is always a pleasure to be around. Chris has fond childhood memories of staying with a favourite auntie in Wiltshire. He knew that he would be spoilt every time he went there. Whereas visits to other relatives could be turgid affairs for an 8-year-old, with all the adults wrapped up in boring adult stuff, he knew that here he would be made to feel special. His auntie would sit with him on a big floral chintz sofa and ask him about his swimming, school and how he was getting on at Cubs. Every answer was greeted with a coo of appreciation which made a little fellow a bit short in self-confidence swell his chest with pride.

His auntie had that priceless gift of making people feel important, and Chris relished the attention, the praise and the recognition of everything that mattered to his 8-year-old world. He walked twice as tall during those visits to Wiltshire where the seemingly endless fields of corn were bathed in mellow sunshine which matched how his auntie made him feel. The fact

---

1   Chris wanted to add Coco Pops but we wouldn't let him!

that he was treated to all his favourites (roast chicken, cola, ice cream), which he never had at home, was just pure bonus! Most precious of all: she gave him her time and he felt valued. She was a wonderful weather god.

Praise and positivity were offered unconditionally. This good soul didn't have to work hard at giving out the praise. She was infused with such a contented view of life that she had a knack of passing it on. She was a natural praiser, imbued with a *joie de vivre* which meant it was a privilege and a pleasure to be in her company. It was a like glorified game of 'pass the parcel' in which every time the music stops, there is another layer of altruism to burnish the cockles of the heart!

# Making it Personal

Not everyone is like Chris's aunt, but we can all aspire to be a similar weather god and unleash our own brand of praise and positivity, constantly in search of new ways to make kids feel good about themselves. In Chapter 4, we began to introduce you to different methods of employing praise in your leadership of schools and classrooms. This chapter takes you further on that journey.

As we have seen, brilliant teachers create the emotional weather in their classrooms. They appear to have the innate gift of conveying to each child the sense that they are valued. This seems obvious and, like all things where you watch an expert at work, it looks easy, but the truth is that it is a skill which can be carefully crafted and developed.

There is a deep-seated desire in all of us to be appreciated and an equivalent dislike of being told off. Sadly, there are many children whose experience of life is one in which they are constantly shouted at and belittled, and almost by default they expect this from their teachers. Many have written off their chances of being successful in at least some subject areas, especially the ones in which they have little apparent natural affinity. Great teachers are the ones who are able to counterbalance this instinctive negativity by using praise to help make kids believe that they can be successful. They are able to inject that factor into pupils' thinking from the moment they enter the learning environment. This can be as simple as a smile or warm words of welcome or a mini-conversation linked to something the teacher knows about the child. The key is that these teachers *show* the pupils they care about them. The kids want to be there because the teacher has made the learning interesting, accessible and worthwhile. Teachers can spin a web of magic, not only in terms of the collective emotional environment they create for the whole class but also in how they make each and every child feel. It is back to our core message about relationships. To pursue the analogy of Chris's auntie, they sit them on the metaphorical chintz sofa where they feel comfortable and valued.

## Clever stuff

Karen Chalk and Lewis Bizo's 2004 study provides us with some clarity on how praise works in schools.[2] The researchers assert that praise is vital in our classrooms and single out *specific praise* in particular.

Specific praise focuses on desired behaviour and links the praise directly to the related outcomes. So, rather than simply saying, 'Well done,' you would say something like, 'Well done, you've really worked hard on your line work over the last two weeks and your drawing is so much better because of it.'

---

2   Karen Chalk and Lewis A. Bizo, 'Specific praise improves on-task behaviour and numeracy enjoyment: a study of year 4 pupils engaged in the numeracy hour', *Educational Psychology in Practice* 20(4) (2004): 335–352.

The benefits of specific praise found in the study included:

+ Pupils were more on task.

+ Praise increased for both academic and social behaviour.

+ Pupils were more settled and more open to challenge, including difficult tasks.

+ Pupils' academic self-concepts were increased.

+ There was greater awareness by the pupils of what they were doing well.

+ Bouncebackabilty increased.

We are particularly keen on the idea that praise can be used to develop 'academic self-concept' because this is a challenge facing many teachers. We don't want youngsters to have boundaries to their learning, but to constantly seek further challenge and have a thirst for self-development.

The study is clear that the use of praise is beneficial in our classrooms. This should encourage teachers both to experiment in increasing the amount of specific praise they use and to encourage their peers to do the same. This could easily form a collaborative continuing professional development programme, which we feel would be helpful to develop (and find the opportunities for) the kind of systematic and automatic praise needed to achieve a positive impact.

Card manufacturers have created a seemingly endless industry out of praise, but here praise transmutes from an instinctive desire to want to make people feel good about themselves into a celebration of achievement. Greetings cards are available for every kind of success in life, from passing exams or getting a new job to passing your driving test. Reaching life's various natural milestones is celebrated, alongside those that we choose for ourselves like First Communions, engagements or wedding days. Of course, there are those who will cock a cynical eye at the shelves of cards designed to suit every one of life's ups and downs, seeing them purely as mercenary self-indulgence. But there is also a deep-seated impulse to enjoy a sense of occasion, to focus on the positive and to pass on that feel-good factor which genuine praise generates.

A key strategy for all weather gods is to catch kids doing the right thing and praise them for it: 'I love the way you have walked in and got your pencil case out ready for work.' 'Jasmine, do you know you've not turned around in your seat today – that's brilliant!' As with the cards, the reasons for cele-bration can be many and varied, but you can praise each and every learner for working hard and link that to the improvements they have made. Some-times you will have to search hard, but even the smallest steps in progress and achievement are worthy of recognition. This doesn't apply only to the kids. What are the qualities you value about your colleagues or members of your team? Do they know this? Have you made a point of telling them?

## Here's a challenge …

Do you find an opportunity during every school day to praise as many of the children you teach as possible? Is that message reaching home? Can you seek out a reason to praise other pupils or repeat praise those you really need in your pocket?

What about your nearest colleagues? Have you found an opening at least once a week to convey to each person your recognition of some-thing they have done well?

We knew of a head teacher who would write personalised Christmas cards to every single employee – the best part of 200 of them. Each one had a tailored message showing appreciation for that particular individual's contribution to the school. There are those who think that at Christmastime it is up to the 'boss' to shower presents on everyone. 'It's the least they can do,' mumble those of a Scrooge-like disposition. We beg to differ. The best Christmas present of all is to know that someone appreciates you. The head also looked for staff doing great things with the kids – from defusing a crisis to creating joy in the classroom – and sent his own homemade brand of card to thank them for their positivity. When this head teacher came to hang up his chalk and leave the school, one colleague let slip that she had kept every single card she had received from him because she valued them so much.

Naturally, we've discussed the beneficial effects of praise on the receiver, but let us just pause for a moment to consider the effects on the giver. Positive outcomes and positive relationships benefit the giver of praise as much as the recipient. Few leaders relish the thought of constantly having to enforce their requirements and expectations against a stone wall of resistance: nothing is more likely to raise the blood pressure and induce undesirable stress.

# Pre-Emptive and Predestined Praise

Between us we have many years of leadership under our belts, and we put it to you that while there are difficult times when you have to sit someone down and have a tough conversation with them, it is equally demanding and draining to conduct a war of attrition with a colleague (or child) with confrontation as a byword. Brilliant leaders and teachers will take the time to reflect on whether there is a way of taking things forward in a creative and altogether more positive way, which will lead to the result they want but minus the aggro and hostility. Both sides win here. Weather gods get to live in warm and sunny climes themselves.

Pre-emptive praise has a clear outcome in mind. It involves praising a child or a colleague for what you want them to do, in anticipation of desirable behaviours or efforts, based on the notion that praise is much more likely to achieve the desired results than rebuke or criticism.

Chris was an old-fashioned parent who insisted that his children hand wrote thank-you letters to family members who had sent Christmas and birthday presents. In theory, Chris's son was on board, but in practice he was a little more hesitant in producing the required goods. This could have developed into a battle royal between two forceful personalities, but Chris took a step back from the fray and asked himself the question, 'How can I get him to want to write his thank-you letters?' *Force majeure* was an option but it would be a pyrrhic victory at best, and using parental authority was a no-no. Different tactics were needed. What Chris actually said was partly fictitious. He told his son, 'Interesting conversation with Uncle George last night. He said he gets so much pleasure from your regular thank-you letters, and that is why he always sends you something for your birthday and for Christmas.' Next morning, job done!

How could this work with a class? A colleague of ours who was new to the school took on a lower ability group for GCSE English, but due to a genuine misunderstanding she thought they were much higher in ability. She taught them throughout the year as if higher in ability than their official designation, praising them for their commitment, their effort and their progress. Guess what? Their results at the end of the year almost mirrored those of the actual higher ability set.

A class teacher Gary observed recently was overseeing the arrival of her class and some of the kids were being a little rowdy and boisterous as they came in. Once they had found their way to their places, she thanked them for remembering that when they came into the class they had agreed rules about behaving calmly and sensibly, and not pushing and shoving. She was thanking them for what she wanted them to do next time. Gary witnessed what happened next time. With only the merest nod from her to remind them of the expectation, they came in beautifully. Lovely weather!

Predestined praise is even more sharply focused. This is where you offer praise as an incentive or a reward for a prescribed goal, along the lines of a nursery assistant saying, 'If you eat all your lunch, I will tell your mum or dad when they come to collect you' (i.e. 'Do this and you will get this!').

This method is used in training animals, whereby a treat is used to establish desired behaviour. Right at the top of most animals' wish list is food and praise from their owner. An owner will therefore reward a dog with a treat or verbal praise which the dog begins to associate with a particular behaviour. When told to sit, the dog will link compliance with the instruction with a doggy treat from the owner's pocket. When training a dog to walk to heel, it may be impractical to stop and reward the dog with a favoured treat, but because dogs crave approval from their owners they will respond equally well to a positive tone of voice.

Of course, there is an alternative method of training involving scolding and physical reprimand. Anyone who has dealt with a puppy who chews up anything it can find when left alone knows that telling them off upon return bears very little fruit. The dog does not link the chewing to the scolding, and quite possibly just sees it as a form of receiving attention, even if it's unpleasant.

# Clever stuff

Far from being a nebulous theory, predestined praise is given credence by John Locke, the renowned seventeenth century philosopher. In his 1690 *An Essay Concerning Human Understanding*, he expounded on his theory of learning being a process of association, and pointed the way towards an understanding of the idea that we make an association between an action and an outcome.[3] For example, a child who is being potty trained will learn that success on the potty leads to praise and celebration, in the same way that a student who invests a huge amount of time in preparing for a test gets to know the glow of satisfaction, praise and success when the exam has gone well.

Ivan Pavlov, the nineteenth century Russian physiologist, took this a stage further with his research into classical conditioning. Having noticed that dogs salivated when they thought they were about to be fed, he pursued the same line of thought as Locke and began to ring a bell when the dogs were about to eat. The dogs began to associate the bell with the food, and over a period of time they began to salivate just on hearing the bell and without the smell of the food.

Both of these thinkers give substance to our thoughts about using praise as a means of getting people to want to do what we want them to do. School teachers know that offering a gold star, a merit or a commendation is a more effective way of getting a child to do homework than a threat or penalty. Punishment may perhaps achieve short term compliance, usually only enough to avoid the punishment. But it will also achieve a resentful falling into line which is unlikely to last or encourage the individual to go the extra mile.

3   John Locke, *An Essay Concerning Human Understanding* (London: Penguin, 1997 [1690]).

The threat of a detention has certainly never made a child want to learn or to do homework. Similarly, the threat of disciplinary action may have a short term impact on a colleague who is falling short of expectations, but it is unlikely to see that colleague grow and thrive, unless supported by a positive incentive and recognition of their efforts to address the concerns.

Mick watched a brilliant teacher working with a pretty challenging and reluctant student in Year 9 recently. Predictably, the kid was late – Jack the lad appeared at the door just as the class were settling into their first task. Far from stopping the class to berate the young man for coming in late, the teacher kept going with his explanation of the task in hand, greeting the latecomer with a 'Hi, great to see you. I was worried you weren't here today,' as he guided him to his seat. While the others were engrossed in the initial activity, the teacher pointed to a merit certificate on the desk in front of the lad. It was specific and targeted and just for him: 'To get a paragraph written by 11.10 a.m.' The pupil didn't immediately conform to the agreed criterion for achieving the reward, so the teacher used it as hook to remind him of what he had signed up to, which was super effective way of getting him back on task. The merit was duly awarded at 11.11 a.m., by which time the boy had produced a pretty decent piece of writing, apparently far in excess of what he normally achieved. By the way, now that vibes of positivity were flowing, the teacher took the opportunity to find out the reason for his lateness.

This teacher was Mr Different. The student was expecting to be told off because that is what he always gets. Instead, he was immediately engaged, he could see what was in it for him and the outcome was better work and better behaviour. No aggravation, no threats of penalty, just positivity and answers to the subliminal question, 'Why should I work for you?' Interestingly, when Mick spoke with the young man at the end of the lesson, his response was, 'I like Sir. He gets me!' Weather god extraordinaire!

Chris took over as line manager of a notoriously difficult colleague who always felt the world was against him. Over a period of time, Chris gained his confidence and respect by making it his business to make sure that he recognised the quality of the teacher's contribution in areas in which he was proficient and telling him so. Hard work and certainly time consuming, but it turned this colleague around and he went on to become a very effective member of the team, exceeding everyone's expectations.

In any relationship, whether it is personal or professional, positivity and praise will oil the wheels much more effectively than criticism, threat and reproach. Praise is always most powerful when it is enticing, immediate and continuous. Does this sound like your school, your staffroom or your classroom? It's no good trying to train a dog with treats it doesn't like, and nor does it make sense, when training a dog to sit, to give them a reward when they have stood up again after perfunctorily bobbing their backside to the floor. The praise needs to be consistent and it should be something they really want.

# Creating a Culture of Positivity

What does this look like in a school situation? Gary's mate at the rugby club was the head teacher at a pupil referral unit (PRU). It's the type of school that expelled kids are sent to and so can be a challenging place to work. This was no job for the faint-hearted. The days can be long (Gary knows this well as he was once seconded for a couple of years to head up a PRU in difficulty) and sometimes staff can feel their efforts are falling on deaf ears. The head was concerned at his inability to retain staff; there was a constant turnover at many levels and the reviews of the school were poor.

Two years back he had introduced a culture of total positivity. This started with the recognition that every single member of the workforce was valuable and indispensable, from the catering staff and cleaners to the office staff, teaching assistants and teachers, right through to the governing body. The first step was that he personally thanked every member of staff at least once a week for something they had done. This was conveyed in person or by text or email. Just good leadership and creating the right weather in the organisation? Maybe. But he went a stage further. Every member of staff was given a card which they had to send to a colleague praising them for something they had done. The praise ranged from how a member of staff had defused a difficult situation with a student to brilliant custard at lunchtime to how brilliantly one member of the premises staff had dealt with Chelsee, who had something of a reputation for not always being completely cooperative when caught sneaking a fag behind the gardeners' hut.

He also introduced 'Kerr-ching' days when colleagues were invited to post a message on a sticky note on the staff noticeboard to celebrate something positive. Then there was a 'Buck's Fizz Week' during which each member of staff drew the name of another colleague out of a hat (Secret Santa style) and then had to find as many ways as possible of praising that person throughout the week without them knowing who their 'admirer' was. Old computers were installed in the corridors on which scrolling positive messages with graphics linked to popular culture were shown for all to see – for example, images of the latest music sensations were overlaid with a positive sentence linked to effort and famous sporting heroes were adorned with a 'can do' quote. The aim was to subliminally influence the kids who passed these images many times daily. Staff were also encouraged to pass on this positivity in the form of praise to the students.

Praise became an endemic part of the school. The outcome? The whole climate changed. Staff retention rates recovered and student behaviour improved. John Locke's association theory in which going to work is associated with success and praise and Pavlov's classical conditioning began to take hold and the institution was transformed. This was predetermined praise with a purpose. Cost in monetary terms: zero. Value in human terms: inestimable.

## Challenge ...

Can you get together with your colleagues, pool your creativity and come up with a similar idea for the teams you work in? Create your own high praise environment between yourselves and see first-hand the power this can unleash.

As we have seen, praise is a great motivator and is an essential part of the toolkit for great teachers to get the best out of kids and colleagues. The outcomes are therefore directly derived from the intentions of the praise giver: the feel-good factor, celebrating success, pre-emptive praise to change the way people see themselves and predetermined praise to reward a specified desired achievement.

However, praise works in mysterious ways. For example, consider how powerful understated praise can be. A well-known lager manufacturer adopted the tag line, 'Probably the best lager in the world'. A masterpiece! The unwritten script was that it was the best lager in the world, but to have said so outright would have been crass, so the desired effect was achieved in a far more subtle way. Overstated praise is almost always counterproductive and makes cynics out of the best of us.

# Getting it Right

There are other dimensions of praise which have an altogether different dynamic. Inappropriate praise will simply backfire and be thrown straight back at the person giving it. There is never any point in flannel when it comes to giving praise. Soft soap doesn't wash. Gary watched a teacher working with a class in a primary school where the children were learning how to draw and paint. The teacher went up to a little boy called Rudi and said, 'That is a great picture, Rudi. I love what you've done!' 'No, it's not, it's rubbish,' retorted Rudi. He didn't like art and thought he wasn't any good at it, which was confirmed by the pictures done by all the children around him, which in his view were all much better than his. When it came to what he regarded as false praise, he was having none of it, and it actually made it harder for the teacher next time when Rudi's work really had come on.

Praise loses its potency when it is sprinkled like confetti. Young Mr Grace in the much loved TV sitcom *Are You Being Served?* is associated with the catchphrase, 'You've all done very well.' He said it every time he visited the shop floor and it was more or less the only thing he said, so it became an empty refrain devoid of meaning. On the Saturday night favourite *Strictly Come Dancing*, Sir Bruce Forsyth would say to each succeeding couple, 'You're my favourites!' Of course, it became a running joke (one of many ascribed to Brucie), but the point is that what was intended as praise lost any credence and as a result was largely ignored.

Chris could give a masterclass to anyone on the subject of acting as a consultant to their wife when it comes to choosing a suitable outfit. Recently, his wife was to accompany him to a prestigious event, so the choice of dress was crucial. She appeared downstairs in option number one: 'You look stunning,' he said. Option number two appeared soon after: 'Stunning, absolutely stunning,' he said. Flushed with her obvious success, Mrs H went upstairs to don outfit number three and, on her reappearance, Chris's verdict was, 'Stunning!' At that point he was rumbled. Effective praise is in the eye of the beholder. If it is fake or overworked, it loses its impact.

In an age of media exaggeration, we are all too painfully aware of those times when praise is heaped and hyped on certain people who promptly vanish from view. The victors of some of the more glitzy talent shows which occupy our television screens on Saturday nights, not to mention the Eurovision Song Contest, typically win in a blaze of glory, never to be heard of again. Many a sportsperson has been blighted by being touted as 'the next

Navratilova/Pelé' and has simply not been able to live up to the expectations piled on them.

So, what lessons can we learn? Weather gods in schools need to ensure that their praise is both genuine and balanced – for example, making it part of the development of a particular child. This means that praise continues to be a sought-after commodity, but one which also helps to build the pupil's learning, creativity and desire for engagement throughout their school life. Kids should not be allowed to be one hit wonders!

Praise can be a fickle friend. Given in the right way, it can uplift and inspire and can literally change the emotional weather; handled in the wrong way, at the wrong time and with the wrong person, it can have the opposite effect (more on this later). Whether at work or at home, praise is either a powerful tool of positivity to be valued and treasured or an unwelcome source of irritation.

## Top tips

- Use pre-emptive praise to encourage desirable behaviours.

- Use predestined praise to prompt desirable behaviours.

- Praise changes the weather and can create a positive feeling in the recipient that can be passed on.

- Be systematic in using praise to build relationships with staff and kids.

- Create your own quirky ways of passing on praise.

# Chapter 6
# Praise Unleashed

> *Praise is like sunlight to the human spirit: we cannot flower and grow without it. And yet, while most of us are only too ready to apply to others the cold wind of criticism, we are somehow reluctant to give our fellow the warm sunshine of praise.*[1]

We agree with Jess Lair that too often our default position in relationships with others is a negative one, but we also share her belief that praise – beautifully described by her as 'sunlight to the human spirit' – can be a powerful motivator. Motivated people are more engaged, and engaged people perform better and gain greater satisfaction from the activity in which they are involved. It stands to reason then, that if we can learn how to use praise in the most effective ways, it will help us in our daily lives. It can help us to motivate our colleagues, our children, our friends and family, fellow team members, the people we work with, the people we work for, the people who work for us. In short, it's a game changer in terms of developing the positive relationships that form the foundations of a culture in which people thrive.

## Motivation

Understanding motivation is a prerequisite for understanding the impact of praise. Fish and chips, salt and vinegar, chilli and chocolate, strawberry and basil, love and marriage, praise and motivation – they go together, a match made in heaven.

---

1   Jess Lair, *I Ain't Much, Baby – But I'm All I Got* (Greenwich, CT: Fawcett, 1976), p. 248.

Psychology recognises two main types of human motivation: extrinsic and intrinsic. Extrinsic motivation occurs when someone is responding to external pressures or tangible rewards. In this way, a colleague may be motivated to work particularly hard because there is the potential for promotion. Similarly, well-placed praise from your head of department can act as an emotional external motivator, and we know that weather gods specialise in this. Conversely, a person may be motivated to work particularly hard at a job to avoid being berated or criticised by the same head of department or any other team leader. In either case, the person is motivated by something extrinsic in their environment.

## Clever stuff

Some psychologists claim that extrinsic motivators are more effective than intrinsic factors. An example of this way of thinking is incentive theory which began to emerge in the 1940s and 1950s. It is based on the thinking of behaviourist psychologists, such as B. F. Skinner, who developed the theory of operant conditioning – the process of changing behaviour using positive and negative reinforcement.[2] Rather than focusing on the more intrinsic forces behind motivation, incentive theory argues that people are primarily extrinsically motivated. Hence, individuals are sometimes pulled towards behaviours that lead to rewards or avoid actions that might lead to negative consequences.

Intrinsic motivation involves engaging in a behaviour for its own sake, for no apparent reason other than the inherent gratification gained from doing it. A student works hard because they get pleasure from learning, satisfaction from being successful and fulfilment from knowing they will be the

---

2   Burrhus Frederic Skinner, *The Behaviour of Organisms: An Experimental Analysis* (New York: Appleton-Century-Crofts, 1938).

best they can be. They are motivated by feelings, ambitions and drivers within themselves.

It has become modern orthodoxy to regard intrinsic motivation as being more effective than extrinsic motivation. While both offer a route to motivation, intrinsic motivation is deemed to be superior because it is linked to desirable outcomes such as improved self-esteem, a greater sense of autonomy and independence, greater resilience and creativity. We suspect that it makes common sense to many of us that adults and children feel better about themselves and grow in self-confidence and determination when they have been praised for a job well done and know that they are appreciated for this. They feel better about themselves and they are driven to work even harder in the future because they enjoy the sense of self-worth and self-esteem this brings. Their motivation and drive to achieve comes from within themselves, and great weather gods know how to ride this wave.

To illustrate this idea, let's take the practical example of Mick in his new part-time volunteering role as a guide for visitors at his local museum. He doesn't get paid, he gives up his own time on a regular basis and he does the job because he enjoys it and gets satisfaction from sharing his passion for history with visitors (his wife calls it lecturing to a captive audience!). On his first day as a guide, the museum curator came to find Mick at the end of the afternoon to praise him for a job well done. He shared with Mick, quietly and privately, how he had received great feedback from visitors about Mick's guiding. His enthusiasm and knowledge had been well received. This made him feel great about himself and what he was doing, and it also motivated him to go off and do even more research and preparation so that in the future he could share ever more interesting bits of the past with visitors. Mick didn't go off and redouble his preparation efforts because he craved repeat recognition from the curator; he did it because it gives him satisfaction to do the job well. His motivation to improve comes from within himself. The simple piece of well-timed and delivered praise fuelled his intrinsic motivation. It's a powerful tool in the classroom and with colleagues too.

In a school setting, we need look no further than the sixth form to find a good illustration of both intrinsic and extrinsic motivation at work. What motivates these young adults to work hard and be resilient when things get tough? To have the personal determination to use their 'private study' sessions to do just that – to choose to study independently in the library for that essay on the causes of the First World War for A level history, when instead they could be tempted by the combination of a bit of study alongside a fair bit of catching up on chatting to friends on social media in the common room? Why choose to stick with their studies when some friends have left school already and are enjoying the material rewards of their first employment?

Mick has lots of experience in sixth forms and of being a one-to-one mentor to sixth form students. He has witnessed a complex range of motivations. At one end are those young people with an internally driven steely determination to succeed because they have a thirst for learning. They are interested in their studies in their own right. They want to push themselves to find out more and understand better. They enjoy being regarded as intellectual and clever. They have ambitions for themselves in the sixth form and want to achieve them. They may well have chosen their future career path and are determined to go to their first choice university to study their first choice course in order to be the successful people they want to be. These youngsters tend to work steadily and don't need constant monitoring and reminding about why they need to study. They are intrinsically motivated to get on and succeed.

The following conversation was related to Mick by the mum of one of his Year 13 girls. Mum and daughter were on a second visit to her first choice university and were walking through the university library on a Saturday afternoon in January. Mum said, 'Look at all these people in the library on a Saturday afternoon. They must have sad lives.' Her daughter replied,

'No, mum, they just want to be successful and achieve.' That sums up an intrinsically motivated young person perfectly.

At the other end of the spectrum are those young people who are motivated by external rewards and pressures. Perhaps they are driven by the prize of a well-paid job at the end of it all, the prospect of letters home praising attendance or effort in lessons, or the possibility of an award at a presentation evening. Or they may be motivated by the fear of letters home to parents with accounts of weak grades, low average attendance and poor effort – the sort of letter which would threaten their place in the sixth form. They are driven either by the fear of punishment or the attraction of reward. These extrinsic motivators may lead to them doing extremely well at school – or, in Mick's experience, they may be more likely to lead to them doing just enough to achieve a degree of success and avoid serious problems but never enough to really do themselves justice. They are simply not motivated enough to do everything required to be really successful.

In today's pressurised education system, it is highly probable that any student, intrinsically motivated or not, will be surrounded and influenced by a range of tools designed to boost extrinsic motivation. These have become standard procedure in almost all schools up and down the country. They will have target grades for every course and regular assessments of academic progress, effort and attitude. Progress letters home and meetings between parents and tutors/mentors/heads of sixth form will follow. Praise flows for those meeting targets and a range of intervention strategies will be deployed for those off target.

We are not being critical of the strategies employed by schools to help students succeed. While there will be students in sixth forms (and colleges) who are solely motivated either by their own inner drive or by a variety of external rewards and inducements, there are many other young people whose drive for success comes from a blend of both intrinsic and extrinsic motivation. Many otherwise intrinsically motivated young people will benefit from the boost of a timely and well-planned extrinsic motivator at certain pressure points in their sixth form career.

# Surely a Bit of Praise Can't Hurt You?

> *Praise, like penicillin, must not be administered haphazardly. There are rules and cautions that govern the handling of potent medicines – rules about timing and dosage, cautions about possible allergic reactions. There are similar regulations about the administration of emotional medicine.*
>
> Haim Ginott[3]

Great weather gods handle praise with care. Let's get this out into the open now: praise can actually work against you if you don't fully understand the power of the tool you are using. But everyone likes a bit of praise, don't they? A pat on the back, a positive word, a trophy, recognition of an achievement? Not necessarily.

---

3    Haim G. Ginott, *Between Parent and Child* (New York: Macmillan, 1965) p. 39.

## More of that clever stuff

It is worth reflecting on David McClelland's human motivation theory (sometimes called the learned needs theory), which is set out in his book *The Achieving Society*.[4] McClelland builds on work from the early 1940s by Abraham Maslow, who formulated the theory of a hierarchy of human needs. It will help to have a simple understanding of Maslow before we consider McClelland.

Maslow first proposed the hierarchy of needs in his 1943 paper 'A theory of human motivation', which identified and described the needs that motivate human behaviour.[5] The hierarchy of needs has five levels: the first level is the basic need for survival comprising necessities such as food and shelter, which is followed by the second need for safety and the third need for love and belonging. The fourth level is esteem, exemplified by the need to be respected. The final level of need is for self-actualisation or fulfilling one's potential.

McClelland built on this hierarchy, identifying three motivators (or drivers) that he believed we all have: (1) a need for achievement, (2) a need for affiliation and (3) a need for power. One of these drivers will be our dominant motivating driver, and this will result from our culture and experiences – that is to say, these are learned and not innate.

It seems quite clear how praise fits in here. What we in schools need to understand is how to identify what the key motivating drivers are for those we want to motivate, and how to tailor make the style and type of praise to fit.

---

4   David McClelland, *The Achieving Society* (Princeton, NJ: Van Nostrand, 1961).
5   Abraham H. Maslow, 'A theory of human motivation', *Psychological Review* 50(4) (1943): 370–396. Available at: http://psychclassics.yorku.ca/Maslow/motivation.htm.

All three of us have used McClelland's and Maslow's ideas about motivating drivers with good results in different contexts, although we would be the first to admit that we haven't always got it right. All of us are parents, we have all taught groups of children and we have all led large teams of people.

Chris, for example, realised that certain key members of his team were motivated by feeling valued, but equally they were resistant to change. He targeted praise bit by bit in such a way that those team members felt valued, and as if they were actually the instigators of the change. He did this by first identifying what the change needed to be and then breaking it down into small non-challenging components. Next, he asked specific individuals to tackle those small components and praised them for their efforts and the outcomes of their work. Then he added more components and so on until the jigsaw pieces came together to create a larger change. He took no credit for this, but continued to reward the targeted team members (who he knew would have been resistant to anything presented as a large shift) as being the driving force behind the team's success.

Our friend and educational genius Sir Tim Brighouse calls this the butterfly effect.[6] He talks about the idea that if enough butterflies were to beat their wings in the Amazon rainforest, the chain of effects would be huge and could cause a tornado in another part of the world. This can be a really useful way of building change while creating a positive ethos: in our experience, the continual dropping of small butterflies into a situation in which you want to see a bigger transformation, coupled with praise for the effort of the people you have targeted, can result in brilliant long term change.

---

6   Sir Tim Brighouse, 'Collecting "butterflies" of good school practice', *Learning Exchange* [blog] (2013). Available at: http://thelearningexchange.org.uk/guest-post-sir-tim-brighouse-butterflies/.

# Last bit of clever stuff!

Any foray into psychological research, theory or literature on praise will invariably focus heavily on studies involving children in education and learning. This is simply because most of the available academic research into praise is in this setting. Those who wish to delve deeper would do well to read a detailed academic paper by Jennifer Henderlong and Mark Lepper who review over thirty years of studies into the effects of praise on children's intrinsic motivation.[7] They come to the conclusion that praise does indeed have an effect on the intrinsic motivation of children; in fact, praise can undermine, enhance or have no effect at all, depending on certain factors. They organise the factors (both positive and negative) that influence the effect of praise on the intrinsic motivation of children into five main areas:

1. Sincerity of the praise given – praise may be perceived as insincere and so could have negative effects.

2. Performance attributions – what does the particular form of praise used lead children to believe are the reasons for their success? Are these things they can control or not?

3. Perceived autonomy – praise can enhance or undermine intrinsic motivation depending on whether it leads children to believe they are in control of their outcomes and responsible for any future success.

4. Competence and self-efficacy – praise can enhance intrinsic motivation when it makes the child perceive themselves as competent and capable of success. It can undermine motivation if based too much on social comparison (competition).

5. Standards and expectations – praise can enhance intrinsic motivation when it sets reasonable and achievable standards and expectations.

---

7   Henderlong and Lepper, 'The effects of praise on children's intrinsic motivation'.

By building on Henderlong and Lepper's research, alongside our wider reading over the years and the insights gained from our combined experience, we have compiled a brief summary of those factors which we think teachers should consider when thinking about using praise to raise the motivation of their pupils. We believe these same factors also apply to teachers' praise of colleagues in the school. We have included some examples of using praise with children and adults to help illustrate this.

# Be Sincere

Let's be honest, praise is not always given for genuinely praiseworthy achievement. But it needs to be, as the kids will work out when you are not being truthful. Or worse, they will become too confident based on your overzealous praise and then become unstuck when they have to prove themselves. This is especially the case in those situations of frequent and regular praise giving which can become a kind of habit or ritual. If praise is delivered out of some kind of social pressure to be seen to be praising colleagues or out of a sense of duty because 'it's expected of managers' and you don't want to be seen as a bad boss, then problems are likely to lay in wait.

Praise that is overly effusive, too general, not person specific, flies in the face of other obvious evidence or is delivered to make someone feel better, but isn't true or credible, will not be perceived (or accepted) as sincere. If praise is felt to be insincere it will have a negative motivational impact. With adults, it can be taken to signify, 'They must want something' or 'It must be Friday afternoon because the boss is out on one of her praising rounds.' Children can spot from a mile off a dose of false praise delivered by a teacher just to get them onside and behaving well. Such cavalier use of something as powerful as praise will not improve motivation and may even cause damage to the overall quality of relationships. So beware the potential perils of false praise. Weather gods treat it like syrup of figs: always give the right dose and for the right reasons, or the consequences could be explosive!

Gary had a small dose of false praise when he tried to learn how to play the guitar. This was something he had wanted to do for many years. As a child growing up in a northern pit village, peer pressure meant you didn't play anything other than football, so despite his mother offering to pay for various music lessons, he caved in and kicked a ball around with his mates. In 1997, at the age of 36, when he finally bit the bullet – buying two guitars and attending weekly lessons – he was determined to put this right and live the dream. He was going to master the guitar and form a band! According to his guitar teacher he was doing well and he was praised regularly. Despite feeling a little awkward, he hung on to his teacher's comments which told him he was progressing well and continued the lessons for nearly two years – until the bombshell! It went something like this:

Gary (guitar in hand): *Can I play you something I've been practising?*

Gary's wife (sitting on the settee): *Go on then.*

(Gary puts foot up on settee like a proper rock guitarist and begins to play and sing 'Love is All Around' by the Troggs; he strums erratically and has to stop to be able to sing the words)

(Gary's wife falls to one side on the settee laughing and lost for words)

Gary: *Bloody hell!* (sulks)

Later that week, Gary put his guitars and associated paraphernalia into the loft. It is still there.

Looking back, Gary is philosophical about the episode (not that he ever neglects the opportunity to remind his wife how she caused him to give up his dream), but wishes that he hadn't been seduced by the praise his teacher handed out. Without doubt, the teacher was a lovely bloke and had Gary's best interests at heart, but the combo of assuming he was making good progress and the humiliation Gary felt when he realised he was actually pretty rubbish has had lasting effects. Three years ago Gary bought a harmonica, thinking he might try to learn how to play it. It is still on a shelf in his study, the box unopened!

# Get your Timing Right

No one would question a parent praising their teenage son for hard work in their studies (remember our triangulation idea?) and it may work as a very positive incentive. However, when would they prefer to receive such an acknowledgement? At home having dinner together as a family, or in a social setting in front of a group of mates? Praise as a reward in the first scenario hopefully leads to a warm, satisfying glow of happiness for the child. The same praise in the second scenario is more likely to produce the heat of embarrassment and fuel a rush to escape the situation. Like most parents of teenagers, Gary could talk to you all night about a bucket load of examples of times when he's made his daughters cringe with some well-meant but badly timed fatherly praise.

Imagine the situation in school when, as team leader, you set out to praise effusively one team member for a particularly brilliant year's work with Year 11, which had a major positive impact on their GCSE results. Can't go wrong, surely? You feel pleased with yourself that you choose to deliver the hearty praise to your team member in front of the rest of their colleagues at the start of a whole departmental meeting on the first day back after the summer holiday. It is only afterwards, when the colleague recoils in horror at your approbation, that you discover that you're not up to date on the team dynamics at work within your own department. In fact, there have been lots of acrimonious exchanges on social media over the summer about individual members of staff and their respective GCSE results. The praise would have been very well received if it had been delivered at a different time and in a different setting. A case of well-meaning praise backfiring badly. If only you had understood your colleagues well enough to get the timing right.

It is important that you know your team and your kids sufficiently well to judge when a piece of well-planned and very public praise will be well received. The key to success is to understand what will be the most effective incentive, and the optimum time of delivery, for the people being praised and motivated. Effective weather gods not only create the climate, they also constantly monitor the weather, judging when it is best to intervene.

# Make it Individualised

Everyone responds differently to praise, so you need to know your target for praise and what works for them. This is summed up beautifully in the phrase, 'Treat employees like snowflakes … Know your employees and tailor your recognition so it produces the greatest impact for each individual.'[8] Jeff Haden may be writing about a business context but the message still applies to teaching. What matters is that your praise technique is customised to get the best out of the individual child you are praising.

A primary teacher friend of ours recalled an experience with a reception child which all teachers would do well to reflect on. This is recounted in the teacher's own words:

> Surprisingly, Millie joined me at the mark-making table where children were writing the graphemes they knew.
>
> 'Can I do some?' she asked.

---

8   Jeff Haden, 'The 9 elements of highly effective employee praise', *Inc.com* (28 March 2012). Available at: http://www.inc.com/jeff-haden/the-9-elements-of-highly-effective-employee-praise.html.

*She wrote four recognisable ones and made up some more. I was thrilled because this was the first time she had actively chosen to do anything like this ... so thrilled that I casually said, 'Hey, I like how you wrote that "t" – you started at the top and the flick is just the right size.'*

*When my attention moved on to another child, Millie took her pen and obliterated every mark she had made and walked away.*

*It was too soon. I had allowed myself to get overly excited by her efforts. Millie had a tough time before she joined us and was being fostered. Her early experiences had left her confused by feelings and emotions, both her own and those of others. Her natural response to such (for her) overt praise was to destroy it and all evidence of it.*

*I had to find another way to praise Millie. Now, I hate a sticker culture but, as it turned out, they worked for Millie, so we used them. Mind you, she would never choose one of the bigger sparkly ones. She always went for one of the little plain ones. I had to make a mistake with Millie in order to better understand her and how to reach her.*

This links right back to what we have said about the importance of knowing your pupils or your colleagues. Children will develop and mature, their contexts will change and their social dynamics will shift, but they will (nearly all) still desire praise, although the method of delivery may need to be revised. Stereotypically, 11-year-olds love public praise. However, by the time they reach 14, many will not be comfortable with it and will prefer something much less public. Knowing your pupils and constantly monitoring them as they grow will help you to focus your praise in the right way for the individual. This applies equally to praising your colleagues.

# Be Clear and Precise

Praise is at its most powerful when it is specific to the person (or people) being praised, the task they are doing, the skill being shown or the effort being expended. Praise which is too generic can leave people confused and unsure how to build on it.

With a colleague: 'Thanks for delivering that piece of INSET – it was just what we needed. It will help us all to focus on our own year groups and feed the information into the school self-evaluation form when we are looking at the children's involvement and well-being levels. It was clearly a useful course for you to go on and you were able to adapt it for everyone here. It would be good if you worked with the support staff next to get them using it too.'

Or with pupils: 'That was a great piece of writing because it was clear, well structured and followed a logical plan.' This goes beyond the general 'great piece of work'. Getting to the heart of the matter and really focusing on what the individual has actually done well, in a sincere and relaxed manner, will ensure the recipient knows the praise is genuine and therefore value it. Also remember that when you are explaining why it is such a good piece of writing, you are conveying your own ideas about standards – what is okay, what is good and what is excellent. Make sure that when you do this your expectations of the child (or your colleague) are ambitious but realistic.

# Focus on What Can be Improved

Cast your mind back to Chapter 4 for this one, and the relative merits of praising ability or effort and person or process. As you will recall, we recommend focusing on effort, linking it to outcome and using it to develop a 'can do' ethos. Not everyone can be the best at art or the fastest runner, but everyone can try hard. As teachers, if we focus on effort we enable success for all. By developing a positive classroom culture, we engage kids fully in their lessons and great learning is more likely to follow.

# Promote a Sense of Autonomy and Independence

Praise may be harmful if it is perceived as controlling and manipulative. 'Well done, Rosie, you have finally reached your twenty-five key words for reading. You can go and choose your sticker now,' might be more effective if it promotes a sense of autonomy in the recipient: 'Rosie, I like the way you've done that – that's a different way to do it.'

Children should believe that they are being praised for something genuine, something they've done through their own talents and effort. In this way they are left feeling empowered and in charge of securing further success in the future. This can be powerful stuff and deliver a real boost in intrinsic motivation of the kind that leaves them wanting to go on and do well for the sake of doing well, and not simply as a means to an end. It's better to praise a child in a way that allows them to understand that they are doing this for themselves and not for their parents/teachers or simply to win more praise. They will then have the self-confidence and desire to take risks and be more innovative.

Consider the following feedback to a Year 5 pupil in a primary school:

*Well done, John, for your piece of work on researching the lives of the Aztec people. You followed the guidance sheet I gave everyone and managed to cover all the topics on the list. What was really good about your work was that you chose to write this up as a story in the first person. That must have taken a lot of time, thought and imagination. You got it just right – your story is very realistic and full of accurate historical detail. It shows a deep level of knowledge about the lives of the Aztecs.*

Here's some homework for you: how do you think John feels getting this feedback? What is he thinking about the next piece of work in this class?

# Highlight Effort Rather Than Success

Competition can be healthy, but not always; similarly, praising children because they come first might sound attractive, and sometimes it is, but not always. We are not advocating a no competition philosophy here, but it is worth remembering that for some children it carries potential problems – namely when they don't win. Instead, it is best to praise in order to encourage children to focus on mastering a skill so that they improve their level of competency for themselves, not in order to do well against their peers. It's better to build up their self-efficacy – their belief in their own ability to succeed at a task – than win a competition. Praise that concentrates too heavily on social comparisons can lead to children having less perseverance when faced with setbacks in mastering a challenge. Ring any bells?

So, to round up this chapter, our collective experience gained from everything we have read, studied and observed over the years, including research and theory, convinces us that praise can be an amazing tool in the hands of a skilled weather god. It can also be of little use, or even backfire and have negative effects, if used carelessly and without thought. Understanding motivation is critical to unlocking the potential of praise.

## Top tips

- Take time to read and find out about the theory behind praise and motivation. Use this to help to reflect on, understand and refine your practice.

- Praise and motivation are directly linked. Make sure you know which type of motivation you are trying to encourage with your praise – intrinsic or extrinsic? Make sure you know the difference.

- Remember that using praise is not guaranteed to be a success. It can enhance, undermine or have no impact depending on the situation and how you use it. Be sure to use praise but do it thoughtfully and with care.

- Remember, everyone is different. You need to take the time to get to know and understand the person and the situation in order to ensure the type of praise you use is the one most likely to secure success.

# Chapter 7
# **Weather Gods**

Schools make a difference for kids. Teachers and other school staff create changes in young lives that can be transformational. We would argue that working in education, especially in direct contact with pupils, is the best and most important job in the world. No doubt you could argue that the medical profession is more important as those folk help to save lives. However, teachers and others in education are in the business of creating people – helping every young person to become the best adult they can be. Teaching is the only profession that creates all the others. You can't have doctors, electricians, pilots or bricklayers without an educational process happening.

This is why it is so important that the climate in every school is one of sunny weather. These are places where joy is brought into the school by weather god staff; where the leaders lead in such a way that they enable the development of a 'can do' ethos; where creativity and risk taking are encouraged and teaching is exciting, engaging and enjoyable; where kids and staff alike look forward to being. Monday mornings are not a drag and the summer holidays are too long for folk in schools where positivity reigns supreme and praise runs through the corridors like blood through veins.

In the UK, from their first year in school until the age of 16, kids spend around 450 weeks at school. That's roughly 11,400 lessons, depending on the school and curriculum plan. Not a lot of time to deliver the whole of the national curriculum and myriad exam syllabuses. And what about all that other stuff – the unwritten pastoral content, how to play nicely, how to communicate and work in a team, how to handle conflict, how to build relationships and so on? Time in school is short and the learning that happens needs to last a lifetime – and you might have noticed that we only get one of those.

This is why schools need to be brilliant places for kids – why we need brilliant teachers, brilliant classroom assistants and brilliant leaders. Kids deserve the best we can give, and in our view the climate comes before the content. For our children to want to learn, to actually buy in to each teacher's brand of education, the weather must be right. We do not live in the bad old days when a twitch of a cane or the thwack of a slipper made the kids conform. Thank goodness too. Educational establishments should be joyous places for kids. They spend the best part of their lives in them from the age of 4 until 16, so they should feel safe, happy and valued while there. For some, school can be a happy second home; for others, sadly, it is the only opportunity to feel that safety and happiness. Either way, there should be no excuses for those working in schools not to create constructive relationships, deliver positivity and praise relentlessly, in such a way that enables young people to thrive and develop.

We live in a data driven, digital and media fuelled world. Far too often, the view in the media is that 'schools aren't as good as they used to be', 'schools aren't as good as they could be', 'schools aren't as good as they should be'. The results at the end of each year are never good enough, and if they have improved then the exams have got easier. Apparently, we need to be more like Finland, Singapore and China! Kids in the UK are tarred with the brush of being the worst ever – challenging, unruly, difficult. Only yesterday, Gary met a fellow dog walker who asked him what he did for a living. The chat got around to Gary having been a teacher. At that point it was as if a dam had burst and all of the aforementioned prejudices flooded out.

We don't see it like that. The kids are the same as when we started teaching. There has never been a golden age of education. Socrates complained about his pupils and so did the ancient Egyptians. Kids are what kids are – learners. And part of that learning is about pushing the boundaries. In schools where it is mostly sunny, there are fewer folk testing those boundaries, mostly because they want to stay in a happy and enjoyable environment. Schools where kids want to be are places that have the best

chance of getting all that content into their little heads. And schools where effort is king are places where everyone can be brilliant.

Back to Haim Ginott then. Teachers, school leaders and everyone else who works in education are weather gods. What kind of weather god will you be? If the dog is sick in your slippers during the night (if you've never experienced such a thing, let us tell you it is not something to relish!), do you take your disgruntlement into school with you? Or do you get your game face on and unleash your god-like powers, taking a smile across the school yard, through the corridor and into your classroom or office? Do you have a cheery word for the kids as you greet them, consistently building those relationships that are the basis of making them want to do what you want them to do? Do you help the premises officer grab the litter that's blowing out of the bin and find humour in the episode? Even when faced with the topic you like teaching least (or your most challenging class or youngster), can you fizz with energy and inspire? Can you become an effort seeking missile, delivering praise, positivity and challenge to help the kids in your school become the best they can be?

We hope so. Kids need school and classroom gods that make great weather!

# Bibliography

*Attitude* (2015). 'Sporting heroes month: Lionel Messi' (28 May). Available at: https://attitude.co.uk/article/6721/sporting-heroes-month-lionel-messi/.

Boyatzis, Richard and McKee, Annie (2005). *Resonant Leadership* (Boston, MA: Harvard Business School Press).

Boyatzis, Richard, McKee, Annie and Johnston, Frances (2008). *Becoming a Resonant Leader: Develop Your Emotional Intelligence, Renew Your Relationships, Sustain Your Effectiveness* (Boston, MA: Harvard Business School Press).

Brighouse, Tim (2013). 'Collecting "butterflies" of good school practice', *Learning Exchange* [blog]. Available at: http://thelearningexchange.org.uk/guest-post-sir-tim-brighouse-butterflies/.

Brown, Rob (2017). 'School's dead, it's the same lessons every day' [video], *BBC* (7 December). Available at: http://www.bbc.co.uk/news/av/stories-42254523/school-s-dead-it-s-the-same-lessons-every-day.

Chalk, Karen and Bizo, Lewis A. (2004). 'Specific praise improves on-task behaviour and numeracy enjoyment: a study of year 4 pupils engaged in the numeracy hour', *Educational Psychology in Practice* 20(4): 335–352.

Cope, Andy and Whittaker, Andy (2012). *The Art of Being Brilliant: Transform Your Life by Doing What Works for You* (Chichester: Capstone).

Dweck, Carol S. (2006). *Mindset: The New Psychology of Success* (New York: Random House).

Dweck, Carol S. (2007). 'The perils and promises of praise', *Educational Leadership* 65(2): 34–39. Available at: http://www.ascd.org/publications/educational-leadership/oct07/vol65/num02/The-Perils-and-Promises-of-Praise.aspx.

Ginott, Haim G. (1965). *Between Parent and Child* (New York: Macmillan).

Ginott, Haim G. (1972). *Teacher and Child: A Book for Parents and Teachers* (New York: Macmillan).

Goleman, Daniel (2016). 'Master the four styles of resonant leadership', *LinkedIn* (26 March). Available at: https://www.linkedin.com/pulse/master-four-styles-resonant-leadership-daniel-goleman.

Goleman, Daniel, Boyatzis, Richard and McKee, Annie (2013). *Primal Leadership: Realizing the Power of Emotional Intelligence* (Boston, MA: Harvard Business School Press).

Green, Sarah (2012). 'The right mindset for success' [interview with Carol Dweck], *Harvard Business Review* (12 January). Available at: https://hbr.org/2012/01/the-right-mindset-for-success.

Haden, Jeff (2012). 'The 9 elements of highly effective employee praise', *Inc.com* (28 March). Available at: http://www.inc.com/jeff-haden/the-9-elements-of-highly-effective-employee-praise.html.

*Harvard Business Review* (2016). 'Why people quit their jobs' (20 September). Available at: https://hbr.org/2016/09/why-people-quit-their-jobs.

Henderlong, Jennifer and Lepper, Mark R. (2002). 'The effects of praise on children's intrinsic motivation: a review and synthesis', *Psychological Bulletin* 128(5): 774–795.

Henriques, Gregg (2012). 'Relational value: a core human need', *Psychology Today* [blog] (23 June). Available at: https://www.psychologytoday.com/blog/theory-knowledge/201206/relational-value.

Kelion, Leo (2016). 'Children see "worrying" amount of hate speech online', *BBC News* (16 November). Available at: http://www.bbc.co.uk/news/technology-37989475.

Kosin, Julie (2016). 'The 20 most memorable Oscar speeches given by women', *Harper's Bazaar* (28 February). Available at: https://www.harpersbazaar.com/culture/film-tv/a10057/best-oscar-speeches-given-by-women/.

Lewin, Kurt, Lippit, Ronald and White, Ralph K. (1939). 'Patterns of aggressive behaviour in experimentally created social climates', *Journal of Social Psychology* 10(2): 271–301.

Locke, John (1997 [1690]). *An Essay Concerning Human Understanding* (London: Penguin).

Lucas, Dan (2015). 'England v Australia: Rugby World Cup 2015 – as it happened', *The Guardian* (3 October). Available at: https://www.theguardian.com/sport/live/2015/oct/03/england-australia-rugby-world-cup-2015-live.

Mairs, Gavin (2016). 'Six Nations 2016: England's Billy Vunipola thriving on Eddie Jones' "love and compassion" ', *The Telegraph* (8 February). Available at: http://www.telegraph.co.uk/sport/rugbyunion/international/england/12147326/Six-Nations-2016-Englands-Billy-Vunipola-thriving-on-Eddie-Jones-love-and-compassion.html.

Martinuzzi, Bruna (2014). 'What our brains look like on praise and criticism', *American Express Open Forum* (1 August). Available at: https://www.americanexpress.com/us/small-business/openforum/articles/what-our-brains-look-like-on-praise-and-criticism/.

Maslow, Abraham H. (1943). 'A theory of human motivation', *Psychological Review* 50(4): 370–396. Available at: http://psychclassics.yorku.ca/Maslow/motivation.htm.

McClelland, David (1961). *The Achieving Society* (Princeton, NJ: Van Nostrand).

Meltzoff, Andrew N. and Brooks, Rechele (2007). 'Eyes wide shut: the importance of eyes in infant gaze following and understanding other minds'. In Ross Flom, Kang Lee and Darwin Muir (eds), *Gaze Following: Its Development and Significance* (Mahwah, NJ: Erlbaum), pp. 217–241.

Mueller, Claudia M. and Dweck, Carol S. (1998). 'Praise for intelligence can undermine children's motivation and performance', *Journal of Personality and Social Psychology* 75(1): 33–52.

Neff, Kristin (2016). 'The space between self-esteem and self-compassion: Kristin Neff at TEDxCentennialParkWomen' [video] (6 February). Available at: https://www.youtube.com/watch?v=IvtZBUSplr4.

O'Connell, Michael (2017). 'TV ratings: Oscars drop to 32.9m viewers, telecast takes a bigger hit with younger set', *Hollywood Reporter* (27 February). Available at: https://www.hollywoodreporter.com/live-feed/tv-ratings-oscars-drop-again-early-numbers-980854.

Phillips, Charles (2015). *50 Leaders who Changed History* (New York: Quantum Books).

Public Health England (2015). *Promoting Children and Young People's Emotional Health and Wellbeing: A Whole School and College Approach* (London: Public Health England). Available at: https://www.gov.uk/government/publications/promoting-children-and-young-peoples-emotional-health-and-wellbeing.

Pulver, Andrew (2017). 'Costing the Oscars: and your bill for the evening is … $44m', *The Guardian* (26 February). Available at: https://www.theguardian.com/film/2017/feb/25/oscars-2017-how-much-does-hollywood-biggest-party-cost-earn.

Rath, Tom and Clifton, Donald O. (2004). 'The power of praise and recognition', *Gallup Business Journal* (8 July). Available at: http://www.gallup.com/businessjournal/12157/power-praise-recognition.aspx.

Seligman, Martin (2011). *Flourish: A Visionary New Understanding of Happiness and Well-Being – and How to Achieve Them* (London: Nicholas Brealey Publishing).

Seppala, Emma and Cameron, Kim (2015). 'Proof that positive work cultures are more productive', *Harvard Business Review* (1 December). Available at: https://hbr.org/2015/12/proof-that-positive-work-cultures-are-more-productive.

Seuss, Dr. (2012 [1954]). *Horton Hears a Who!* (London: HarperCollins).

Skinner, Burrhus Frederic (1938). *The Behaviour of Organisms: An Experimental Analysis* (New York: Appleton-Century-Crofts).

Smith, Gregory P. (2013). 'Why people quit their jobs', *Business Know-How* (20 May). Available at: http://www.businessknowhow.com/manage/whyquit.htm.

Strand, Steve (2008). Keynote presentation to the National Conference on Tackling Boys' Underachievement, Earls Court, London, 17 June.

Syed, Matthew (2017). *The Greatest: What Sport Teaches Us About Achieving Success* (London: John Murray).

Tickle, Louise (2015). 'Cash for grades: should parents reward exam results?', *The Guardian* (25 June). Available at: https://www.theguardian.com/education/2015/jun/25/cash-for-grades-should-parents-reward-exam-results.

Toward, Gary, Henley, Chris and Cope, Andy (2015). *The Art of Being a Brilliant Teacher* (Carmarthen: Crown House Publishing).

# About the Authors

Gary Toward, Mick Malton and Chris Henley have taught, led and supported schools in a variety of contexts and local authorities across the UK. All three consider teaching to be the most important and most rewarding profession there is. Chris and Gary now deliver keynotes and workshops internationally as part of their business, Decisive Element Ltd.

Chris and Gary are co-authors of the bestselling and highly acclaimed Art of Being Brilliant series. Gary is also a novelist. His first book, *The Magpie*, is a crime novel set during the First World War.

Mick is an educational consultant and joins Chris and Gary in presenting whenever he can. All three have a passion for education and for helping those to whom we entrust the future prospects of our most precious resource: our children. They draw their inspiration from the amazing people who work tirelessly in our schools, changing young lives for the better. This book is a tribute to them.

# The Art of Being a
# Brilliant Middle Leader

## Gary Toward, Chris Henley and Andy Cope

ISBN: 978-178583023-5

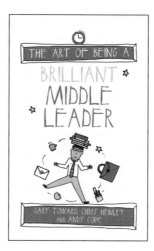

2017 FINALIST

Whether you're already leading or you have it on your radar, this book's for you. Don't expect a textbook full of highfalutin theories though, this book is rammed full of practical ideas that you can use instantly to help you in your current role or to get the position you want. How do you create a brilliant team? What is needed to establish an awesome ethos? How do you do those difficult personnel things? How do you make an impact? Answers to all of these questions and more are based on the combined seventy plus years of the authors' leadership experience in a wide range of educational settings. You'll find a cornucopia of pick and mix tips, strategies and stuff that really works and will make your leadership brilliant!

# The Art of Being a Brilliant Classroom Assistant

Gary Toward, Chris Henley and Andy Cope

ISBN: 978-178583022-8

2017 **FINALIST**

Based on the authors' combined seventy plus years of experience, *The Art of Being a Brilliant Classroom Assistant* is packed full of creative tips, techniques and strategies for anyone with the crucial role of supporting kids' learning. There are many different names and acronyms for these amazing classroom practitioners: teaching assistants (TAs), learning support assistants (LSAs), cover supervisors, supply teachers, student mentors, higher level teaching assistants (HLTAs), learning partners – the list goes on. The job title doesn't matter but the quality of support, interaction and learning does. Whether you work one-to-one with individual children, support small groups or work with a whole class – and whether you work in a primary, secondary or special setting – this book is packed with ideas to enhance your practice so you can best support children's learning, while looking out for your own well-being and enjoying your role.

# The Art of Being a Brilliant NQT

Gary Toward and Chris Henley,
edited by Andy Cope

ISBN: 978-184590940-6

Everything an NQT always wanted to know about starting their teaching career but never dared to ask!

This book will take the NQT through a journey which starts with interviews, leads them through the first visit before taking up the job and then into the first hectic weeks and months. Light in touch but rich in content, it can be read around the pool during the holidays before the start of term or kept by the bedside or in a desk drawer for an emergency flick through once teaching gets under way! It expands on the stuff that teacher training touches on, but importantly provides a refreshing look at the nitty-gritty stuff that most training doesn't!

# The Art of Being a Brilliant Teacher

Gary Toward, Chris Henley and Andy Cope

ISBN: 978-184590941-3

2017 FINALIST

Teaching is an art; with the right techniques, guidance, skills and practice, teachers can masterfully face any situation the classroom could throw at them. With their fresh perspectives, sage advice and a hint of silliness, Gary, Chris and Andy show teachers how to unleash their brilliance.

For any teacher who has ever had a class that are angels for colleagues but Lucifer incarnate as soon as they cross the threshold of their classroom. Or who realised too late that their best-laid lesson plans were doomed from the start. Or who had their energy and enthusiasm sapped by a mood-hoovering staffroom Grinch. These problems will be a thing of the past once they've mastered the art of being a brilliant teacher. With plenty of practical advice and top tips, this book will show them how.